THE TIDE OF WAR

THE 1814 INVASIONS
OF UPPER CANADA

UPPER CANADA PRESERVED
WAR OF 1812

THE TIDE OF WAR
THE 1814 INVASIONS
OF UPPER CANADA

RICHARD FELTOE

DUNDURN
TORONTO

Editor: Cheryl Hawley
Design: Jennifer Scott
Printer: Webcom

Library and Archives Canada Cataloguing in Publication

Feltoe, Richard, 1954-, author
     The tide of war : the 1814 invasions of Upper Canada / Richard Feltoe.

(Upper Canada preserved, War of 1812)
Includes bibliographical references and index.
Issued in print and electronic formats.
ISBN 978-1-4597-1410-6 (pbk.).--ISBN 978-1-4597-1411-3 (pdf).--ISBN 978-1-4597-1412-0 (epub)

1. Canada--History--War of 1812--Campaigns. 2. Canada--History--War of 1812--Battlefields. I. Title. II. Series: Feltoe, Richard, 1954- . Upper Canada preserved War of 1812.

FC442.F436 2013   971.03'4   C2013-904118-4   C2013-904119-2

1   2   3   4   5   17   16   15   14   13

Conseil des Arts du Canada   Canada Council for the Arts   Canada   ONTARIO ARTS COUNCIL CONSEIL DES ARTS DE L'ONTARIO

We acknowledge the support of the Canada Council for the Arts and the Ontario Arts Council for our publishing program. We also acknowledge the financial support of the Government of Canada through the Canada Book Fund and Livres Canada Books, and the Government of Ontario through the Ontario Book Publishing Tax Credit and the Ontario Media Development Corporation.

Visit us at
Dundurn.com | @dundurnpress | Facebook.com/dundurnpress | Pinterest.com/dundurnpress

Dundurn
3 Church Street, Suite 500
Toronto, Ontario, Canada
M5E 1M2

Gazelle Book Services Limited
White Cross Mills
High Town, Lancaster, England
LA1 4XS

Dundurn
2250 Military Road
Tonawanda, NY
U.S.A. 14150

This book is offered:

First, as a salute to the memory of all those, on both sides of the lines, who served, sacrificed, and died as they loyally obeyed their country's call-to-arms in the North American War of 1812–1815.

Second, as a mark of respect to the men and women of the military services of Canada, Great Britain, and the United States, who today honorably continue that legacy of service and sacrifice at home and across the globe.

Third, as a thank-you to my fellow "Living History" reenactors, with and against whom I've "fought" for so many years.

Finally, as a memory from "Bamp" to my grandsons, Anthony, Lawrence, and Daniel.

TABLE OF CONTENTS

Acknowledgements   9

Preface   11

Chapter 1:   Introduction   13

Chapter 2:   Dealing a New Hand and Upping the Ante   20

Chapter 3:   The Winter of Discontent in the West   42

Chapter 4:   Marching in a New Direction — Or Two   63

Chapter 5:   The Attack That Never Was   68

Chapter 6:   The Raid on Oswego, May 5–6, 1814   76

Chapter 7:   Building a New Army   89

Chapter 8:   The Invasion of July 1814   98

Chapter 9:   The Battle of Chippawa   115

Chapter 10:   The High Tide   140

Notes   148

Selected Bibliography   151

Index   156

ACKNOWLEDGEMENTS

As this series moves into book four, the list of those deserving of thanks for their contributions and support grows ever longer. Unfortunately, there is never enough space to adequately recognize every individual by name, and for this I wholeheartedly apologize. However, as in the past, certain people have made exceptional efforts to support this project and it would be remiss of me not to at least recognize them. First and foremost would be my wife, Diane, who manages the business end of things and continues to tolerate and accept my ongoing absences and hermit-like seclusion when I'm upstairs in the "computer" room, writing for hours on end.

Second is Major John Grodzinski, assistant professor in the department of history at the Royal Military College of Canada in Kingston, Ontario, who took time from his already full schedule to read and critique this manuscript and provided valuable insight and vital corrections of interpretive error on my part as it applied to the events surrounding General Prevost and the events in Kingston, Sackets Harbor, and Oswego.

Third, thanks go to my fellow historians Pat Kavanagh and Donald Graves for the work they have done before me, providing me with a valuable trail of research that I have been able to refer to as comparisons to what I have accumulated in my own researches; not to mention the other dedicated staff members of the numerous museums, archives, and libraries that I visited to research this work and who cheerfully assisted me in my searches. Nor can I fail to acknowledge the continued guidance and support provided by my editor Cheryl Hawley, my designer Jennifer Scott, as well as the whole creative team at Dundurn Press, in turning this idea into a reality.

Penultimately, to Barry Penhale and Jane Gibson of Natural Heritage publications and the memory of Karen, who collectively put my feet on the path that allowed me to become an author.

Finally, I want to go on record in expressing my deepest gratitude and thanks to all my readers, who have supported me by buying my books, overwhelmed me by their kind reviews and complements on the series so far, and provided suggestions for ensuring the upcoming parts maintain their deservedly high expectations.

PREFACE

VARIATIONS

As more fully outlined in the introduction to the first book in this series, *The Call to Arms*, the historic material included here includes variations in spelling, jargon, and place-name changes that have occurred over time. As a result, the following standards have been applied.

- Where variations on spelling in quotes are found, the material has been repeatedly checked to ensure its accuracy and is presented just as it was found in the original documents and without the term [*sic*].
- While generally recognized military terms are presented as is, some of the more archaic or jargon-type words are followed by a modern equivalent word. In a similar manner, maintaining the differential identification of military units from the two principal combatant nations (when both used a system of numbers to designate their regiments) has been achieved by showing British Regimental numbers as numerals (41st Regiment., 89th Regiment, etc.) and, where required, with their subsidiary titles (1st [Royal Scots] Regiment, 8th [King's] Regiment), whilst the American Regiments are expressed as words (First Regiment, Twenty-Fifth Regiment, etc.)
- Where place names appear with a number of variants (e.g., Sackett's Harbour, Sacket's Harbour, Sakets Harbor, or Sacket's Harbor) I have adopted a single format for each case, based upon a judgment of what I felt was

the predominant version used at the time. Where names have changed entirely, or would cause needless confusion (Newark becoming Niagara and currently Niagara-on-the-Lake), I have generally gone with what would clarify the location and simplify identification overall or included a reference to the modern name (Crossroads becoming Virgil).

Finally, in including images where there is both a period and modern image combined for a then-and-now effect, I have tried, as far as possible, to obtain the same relative perspective; subject to the limitations imposed where the physical landscape and property ownership make it possible to do so.

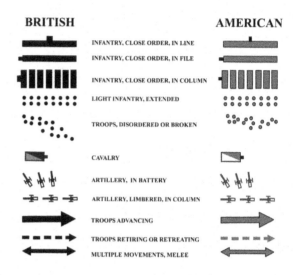

BRITISH		AMERICAN
	INFANTRY, CLOSE ORDER, IN LINE	
	INFANTRY, CLOSE ORDER, IN FILE	
	INFANTRY, CLOSE ORDER, IN COLUMN	
	LIGHT INFANTRY, EXTENDED	
	TROOPS, DISORDERED OR BROKEN	
	CAVALRY	
	ARTILLERY, IN BATTERY	
	ARTILLERY, LIMBERED, IN COLUMN	
	TROOPS ADVANCING	
	TROOPS RETIRING OR RETREATING	
	MULTIPLE MOVEMENTS, MELEE	

CHAPTER 1

Introduction

Between 1808 and 1812, growing international tensions over a catalogue of issues pitted the United States and Great Britain against each other, leading to the spectre of war breaking out between the two nations; a circumstance actively endorsed by a group of political activists within the United States collectively known as "War Hawks." Their goals finally came to fruition in the summer of 1812, when President James Madison signed the declaration of war on June 18, 1812. However, contrary to the prophetic boasts of these War Hawks, the desired war did not go smoothly toward a swift conclusion and the glorious victory they had expected. Instead, it dragged on and degenerated into a year and a half of half-baked campaigns and battlefield defeats at the hands of an alliance of British regular troops, Canadian militia units, and

U.S. President James Madison.

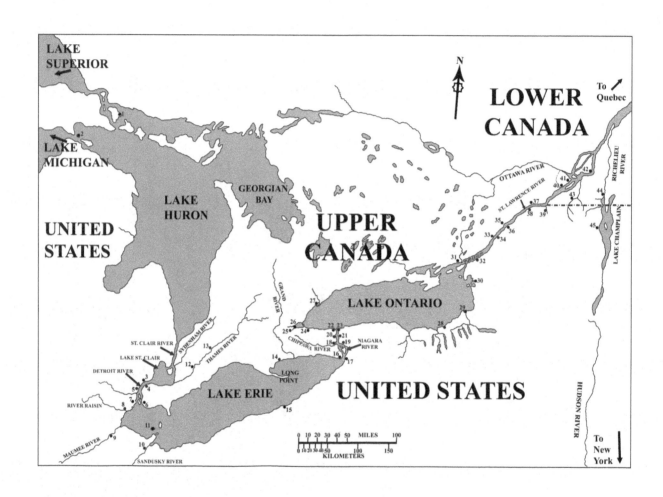

The "Northern Frontier" of the War of 1812–1815.
(Modern Name)   [Fortifications]

1. St. Joseph Island [Fort St. Joseph]
2. Michilimackinac Island (Mackinac) [Fort Mackinac/Fort Michilimackinac]
3. Detroit [Fort Detroit]
4. Sandwich (Windsor)
5. Monguagon/ Maguaga
6. Amherstburg (Malden) [Fort Amherstburg]
7. Brownstown
8. Frenchtown
9. Perrysburg [Fort Meigs]
10. [Fort Stephenson]
11. Put-in-Bay
12. Moravianstown
13. Longwoods
14. Port Dover
15. Presque Isle (Erie, PA)
16. Fort Erie [Fort Erie]
17. Buffalo and Black Rock
18. Chippawa
19. [Fort Schlosser]
20. Queenston
21. Lewiston
22. Newark (Niagara-on-the-Lake) [Fort George, Fort Mississauga]
23. [Fort Niagara]
24. Stoney Creek
25. Ancaster
26. Burlington Heights (Hamilton, ON)
27. York (Toronto) [Fort York]
28. Sodus
29. Oswego [Fort Oswego]
30. Sackets Harbor [Fort Tompkins, Fort Volunteer, Fort Pike]
31. Kingston [Fort Frederick, Fort Henry]
32. French Creek
33. Elizabethtown/ Brockville (1813)
34. Morrisburg
35. Prescott [Fort Wellington]
36. Ogdensburg
37. Crysler's Farm
38. Hamilton (Waddington, NY)
39. French Mills
40. Coteau-du-Lac
41. Cedars
42. Montreal
43. Châteauguay
44. Île aux Noix
45. Plattsburg

Native Allied warriors (hereafter, British or Allies). With embarrassing regularity, the inherent weaknesses of the pre-war American military structure revealed itself to include:

- A senior field command structure principally made up of incompetents and/or geriatrics, appointed for their personal and political connections rather than battlefield expertise.
- A mid-level field command structure composed principally of keen but relatively inexperienced younger officers.
- A governmental administration of the military run by political appointees and insiders, who repeatedly interfered in every level of decision making and even altered the campaign decisions of the field commanders by issuing bureaucratic dictates from the safety of Washington.
- A field-level regular fighting force that was initially made up of inexperienced and half-trained troops, backed by a state militia system that ran upon a virtually independent and sometimes self-serving or competing series of objectives.
- A military supply system that was rife with administrative corruption and fraud, and suppliers that produced and sold substandard military goods at inflated prices and then regularly failed

to deliver in time or in sufficient quantities to fulfill the needs of the troops.

While certain individual military commanders certainly did make substantial improvements in their own commands, nonetheless, by the end of 1813 the overall state of affairs in pressing their war aims was so bad that, on December 31, the American House of Representatives established a Congressional committee of inquiry "requesting such information (not improper to be communicated) as may tend to explain the causes of the failure of the arms of the United States on the Northern frontier ..."[1] from the secretary of war, John Armstrong. A month later, Armstrong responded with a fifty-page document that included transcripts of letters and official reports that catalogued the military debacles at Detroit, Queenston, Frenchman's Creek, Stoney Creek, Fort George, Fort Niagara, Black Rock, Buffalo, Châteauguay, and Crysler's Farm (to name but a few). On the other hand, Armstrong's report, while hinting at the issues outlined above, failed to present any real conclusions or recommendations as to how these failures could be remedied.

The previous books of this series, *The Call to Arms*, *The Pendulum of War*, and *The Flames of War*, have traced the course of those campaigns through 1812 and 1813, as it applied to the Northern frontier.

U.S. Secretary of War John Armstrong.

For those who have not read these earlier works, the following is an abridged timeline of that period.

TIMELINE

- June 17/18, 1812: [Washington] The U.S. Senate passes the vote to declare war on Great Britain. President Madison signs the declaration of war.

- July 12, 1812: [Detroit frontier] U.S. forces launch an invasion of Upper Canada at Sandwich (Windsor) that within weeks withdraws back to Detroit.
- August 16, 1812: [Detroit frontier] Allied forces under Major General Brock, supported by Native allies under Tecumseh, intimidate Brigadier General Hull into surrendering his entire garrison at Detroit.
- October 13, 1812: [Niagara frontier] The Battle of Queenston Heights. U.S. forces invade Upper Canada at Queenston. Major General Brock is killed while leading a counterattack. Later in the day, Major General Roger Sheaffe arrives with reinforcements and leads a successful flanking counterattack upon the American position, routing their line.
- November 28, 1812: [Niagara frontier] The Battle of Frenchman's Creek. U.S. forces make a failed attempt to create a bridgehead for invasion at Fort Erie and Frenchman's Creek.
- April 27, 1813: [Upper Canada] The Battle of York (Toronto). U.S. forces mount an amphibious attack and capture York (Toronto). As they retreat, the British explode their main magazine, inflicting heavy casualties on the American forces. In retaliation, the Americans burn the town's public buildings (Parliament) and Fort York.

- May 1–9, 1813: [Detroit frontier] The Siege of Fort Meigs. Allied forces mount a pre-emptive campaign to destroy Fort Meigs. Although the siege fails, the expedition cripples American plans to mount a counter invasion upon western Upper Canada for several months to come.
- May 27, 1813: [Niagara frontier] The Battle of Fort George. U.S. forces mount an amphibious invasion on the Niagara frontier with an attack on Newark (Niagara-on-the-Lake). Defeated Allied forces are forced to abandon Fort George and retreat to Burlington Heights/Head-of-the-Lake (Hamilton).
- May 29, 1813: [Lake Ontario] The Battle of Sackets Harbor. Allied forces mount an unsuccessful amphibious attack on Sackets Harbor.
- June 6, 1813: [Niagara frontier] The Battle of Stoney Creek. Allied forces make a surprise night attack on advancing U.S. forces encamped at Stoney Creek. Although a tactical draw, the American invasion stalls and the Americans retreat to a militarized enclave around Fort George/Newark.
- June 24, 1813: [Niagara frontier] The Battle of Beaver Dams. U.S. forces being besieged at Fort George attempt a large-scale sortie to disrupt the British outpost at Beaver Dams. Lax security while on the march allows Laura Secord to

bring word to the British, who use their Native allies to entrap and defeat the American sortie.

- July 11, 1813: [Niagara frontier] British forces attack and overrun the American positions at Black Rock.
- July 17, 1813: [Niagara frontier] U.S. forces make a strong probe on the British positions at the Crossroads (Virgil). This engagement represents the first significant action to include Native forces fighting on both sides.
- August 24, 1813: [Niagara frontier] British forces make a sortie against the American positions around Fort George.
- September 10, 1813: [Lake Erie] The Battle of Lake Erie. American naval forces defeat and capture the British squadron on Lake Erie.
- September 23, 1813: [Detroit frontier] Following the loss of the British fleet on Lake Erie and in the face of an American invasion, British forces on the Detroit frontier are forced to destroy their fortifications and retreat north toward the Thames River, pursued by the Americans.
- October 5, 1813: [Upper Canada] The Battle of the Thames/Moraviantown. U.S. forces rout the retreating Allied forces and kill Tecumseh. Western Upper Canada now effectively falls under American hands, while the British continue their retreat to Burlington Heights.
- October 9, 1813: [Niagara frontier] British forces

blockading Fort George abandon their positions and begin a retreat to Burlington Heights.

- October 26, 1813: [Lower Canada] The Battle of Châteauguay. U.S. forces invade Lower Canada, but are repulsed at Châteauguay.
- November 3, 1813: [St. Lawrence frontier] U.S. forces begin a campaign against Lower Canada by sailing an invasion fleet out of Lake Ontario into the St. Lawrence River, which is subsequently pursued by a British force.
- November 11, 1813: [St. Lawrence frontier] The Battle of Crysler's Farm. U.S. forces are defeated by the British at Crysler's Farm, effectively ending the attempted American campaign to attack Montreal.
- December 12, 1813: [Niagara frontier] U.S. troops at Fort George abandon the Canadian side of the Niagara River. Canadian renegades, fighting with the Americans, burn down Newark (Niagara-on-the-Lake).
- December 19, 1813: [Niagara frontier] The Capture of Fort Niagara. British troops cross the Niagara River and mount a surprise night-attack on Fort Niagara, capturing the fort.
- December 29, 1813: [Niagara frontier] The Assault on Buffalo. British forces attack and rout American troops at Buffalo, burning all military positions and civilian dwellings in retaliation for the previous American burning of Newark.

It is now the intention of this work, *The Tide of War*, to take up that story at the beginning of the winter of 1813–14 and begin the account of how the final year of the war developed in the fight to control Upper Canada, and in particular, how the already devastated lands bordering the Niagara River became the location for some of the hardest fought and bloodiest battles, as well as the longest siege recorded during the entire course of the North American War of 1812–15.

Richard Feltoe

CHAPTER 2

Dealing a New Hand and Upping the Ante

Following the intensive and violent events on the St. Lawrence and Niagara frontiers at the end of 1813, the first months of 1814 were, by comparison, a period of little active campaigning. However, behind the scenes there was a massive amount of simultaneous planning and strategizing taking place by the principal players on both sides of the frontier. In addition, as the weeks passed there developed an increasing parallel tempo of construction of new military fortifications, supply warehouses, and barracks to prepare for the approaching campaigns on land, as well as the construction of two enlarged naval fleets to contest the control of Lake Ontario and the St. Lawrence River. Both sides made substantial increases to the volumes of military and ancillary supplies that were ordered, produced, transported, and stockpiled

during this period. Gone were the days of minor probes, amateurish raids, and ill-supplied expeditions. Instead, an entirely new scale of warfare was to be undertaken, as both sides were determined to make the 1814 campaign the decisive blow that would cripple or entirely defeat their enemy — once and for all.

For Lieutenant General Gordon Drummond, the senior British military commander in Upper Canada and lieutenant governor/president of the province's civilian administration, the neutralization of the American military threats on the Niagara and St. Lawrence frontiers at the end of 1813 enabled him to plan for an offensive campaign in 1814. To this end, Drummond followed the same line as his military/civilian administrative predecessors, by making strong representations

G.T. Berthon, artist, c. 1882, Archives of Ontario, Acc. 693127.

Lieutenant General Gordon Drummond.

S.W. Reynolds, artist, date unknown, Library and Archives Canada, C-19123.

Sir George Prevost (commander in chief, British Forces, and governor general, British North America).

to his senior military commander (who was also the governor general of the Canadian colonies), Sir George Prevost, to send additional troops and resources into Upper Canada, where all of the significant fighting over the previous year and a half had taken place. Drummond reasoned that these additional resources were essential if he was to expel the occupying American land forces from the western portions of the province and re-establish his line of communication with the isolated British garrison at Fort Michilimackinac (Fort Mackinac) in the far north. This was to be followed by a period of reconstruction and strengthening of both the existing military depots above Kingston, as well as constructing new shipbuilding centres on Lake Erie for the production of a new British flotilla that would regain the essential transport lines and naval supremacy on that lake. For this latter project Drummond knew he already had the backing of Sir James Yeo, the senior naval commander on Lake Ontario, as Yeo had already proposed a similar project to Prevost the previous December.

To secure his southern flank and prevent any American interference in this plan, Drummond also proposed establishing a strong mobile infantry force at Long Point to guard against any American landing aimed at destroying the planned shipyards, or cutting off his troops on the Niagara frontier, as well as protecting the vital food supplies provided by that area. Finally, he proposed making a daring three-pronged offensive. First, Yeo would lead a force of around two hundred sailors and troops in a march across the frozen Lake Erie to destroy or capture that part of the American fleet that was wintering at Put-in-Bay. At the same time, he (Drummond) would command two columns of troops (cumulatively made up of a total of 750 regulars, 250 militia, 100 Royal Marines, 40 Royal Marine artillery with three field pieces, 400 Native allies, and 20 provincial cavalry) to recapture Amherstburg and seize any American boats wintering there.[1]

In response, Sir George Prevost, while giving an initial qualified approval for this combined offensive operation, continued to expound his own absolute conviction that the American troops wintering along the Lake Champlain and St. Lawrence corridors represented a significant military threat to Lower Canada that negated any argument to send troops into Upper Canada:

From Pictorial Field Book of the War of 1812.

Sir James Yeo (British senior naval commander, "Great Lakes").

... nor indeed is it much my wish to draw the attention of serious exertions of the enemy against that quarter [the Detroit corridor] where we have experienced so much difficulty in forwarding the necessary supplies and from total want of accommodation for carrying on the service ... besides other considerations of a still more important nature, induce me to encourage the enemy in selecting a less distant scene of action for the ensuing campaigns But under every circumstance, the unequivocal demonstration ... of directing their whole disposable force with their utmost energy against Lower Canada must be as unequivocally done away before I can feel myself qualified in making any alteration in the disposition of the troops below Kingston.... The defence of Lower Canada [is] ... a consideration which must never be lost sight of and to which every other, as of minor importance, must give way.... The suggestion of moving a Corps for the recovering our lost position at Detroit is ... beyond our means.... One great objection to detaching Corps [from Quebec] to the distant points of the Upper province is that we thereby expose them to a most arduous and critical struggle without the means of supporting or withdrawing them, while we leave ourselves, by such measures, weak and without a disposable force.[2]

— Prevost to Drummond,
January, 5, 1814

However, Prevost's lack of support became moot when the weather chose not to co-operate with Drummond's plans, as a fluctuating period of unseasonably warm and cold conditions rendered the Lake Erie ice too thin for an infantry attack to be made, but thick enough to prevent any boats being sailed across without the grave danger of striking ice floes and sinking. Consequently, by the end of February, Drummond was forced to call off the entire expedition. Which perhaps was just as well, for there were plenty of additional matters that required his attention, the most immediate being the lack of provisions and supplies with which to feed his army and all of the refugee Native allies he was responsible for. Consequently, Drummond took the extraordinary step of making an extensive personal tour of inspection of the Grand and Upper Thames river valleys during the first weeks of March to assess the potential resources of food and provisions that could be expected to flow from that area. Upon his return, a far more sombre commander penned his findings to Prevost:

> I availed myself of an opportunity to visit that part of the district which lies to the westward, as far as the Delaware town on the River Thames and Long Point and vicinity on Lake Erie. I was much concerned to find that part of the country bordering on the River Thames extremely drained of resources, so much so in fact, as to make it almost amounting to an impossibility to support an adequate force for its protection without drawing all supplies for that purpose from the neighbourhood of Long Point.[3]
> — Drummond to Prevost,
> March 5, 1814

Shortly thereafter, the situation for the provision of grain for the making of bread was deemed so serious that despite the inevitable negative backlash of public opinion, Drummond was forced to issue the following edict:

> York, March 14, 1814 ...
> Know ye that finding it at present expedient and necessary ... I hearby ... prohibit the distillation of spirits, strong waters or low wines from any wheat, corn, or other grain, meal or flour within this Province ... to the first day of July now next ensuing, under the penalties and forfeitures by the said act imposed.[4]

At another level, due to a deficiency in hard cash within Upper Canada, the main medium of currency had devolved upon army-issued bills of exchange or "scrip," which was not meant for widespread circulation within the civilian economy. As a result, commodity prices soared as people began to hoard their gold and silver coinage, whilst simultaneously refusing to be paid in the scrip, thus substantially reducing products and produce being offered for sale to the commissariat and quartermaster departments. This issue also had unexpected fallout on the reconstruction work required to prepare the Niagara frontier fortifications of Fort Erie, Fort Chippawa, Queenston, Fort Mississauga, and Fort Niagara for active service, once the campaigning recommenced in the spring.

Right: (Above) Fort Niagara as seen in 1814, with the roofs of the "French Castle" and redoubts removed to create elevated artillery positions. Note the dilapidated condition of the wooden picket wall on the right and the collapsed segments closer to the lake (left).

(Below) Almost the same perspective in 2012.

Fort Niagara, J.H. Slade, artist, c. 1814, Library and Archives Canada, C-42570.

The first three were essentially fire-gutted and partially demolished shells, capable of no defensive stand if attacked, while Fort Mississauga was only just in the process of being built. Fort Niagara's buildings were essentially intact, but its external earthworks and picketing defences were in a bad state, as a series of land-slips had caused entire sections to cant over or collapse. While the various garrison troops could be ordered to do some of the manual work on these locations, qualified military engineers and skilled tradesmen were in short supply to do the professional jobs. Hiring civilian contractors and workmen was essential if these fortifications were to be repaired. Unfortunately, as these civilian individuals were already in high demand for other civilian work and military projects (such as those under Yeo at Kingston), few were available for work on the Niagara, and those who were available did not like being paid in scrip. The situation became so bad that, as there were not enough trade workers available to produce new picketing to restore the Fort Niagara defences, Lieutenant General Drummond was forced to authorize the dismantling of the picketing already installed at Fort George and its transportation and re-erection at Fort Niagara! Nor could he accede to the recommendation of the region's commander of the "Right Division," Major General Riall, for either the substantial reduction in the scale and dimensions of Fort Niagara defence perimeter (so as to reduce the structural maintenance required and the garrison of troops needed to defend it) or its entire demolition, as Drummond believed that:

> ... although a considerable proportion of the Right Division will necessarily be employed for its defence, yet a still much greater force of the enemy must unavoidably be engaged in its investment, which force might otherwise be at liberty to act against us in perhaps a far more vulnerable point.[5]
>
> — Drummond to Prevost,
> March 22, 1814

In yet another matter, denied the service of additional regular troops from Lower Canada, Lieutenant General Drummond was forced to look to the Upper Canada militias for his new supply of manpower. He therefore revised the regulations upon which his only full-time militia regiment, the Incorporated Militia of Upper Canada, was operating.

Having been formed the previous March, the original intention had been to establish three full battalions of this corps. Unfortunately, insufficient volunteers had stepped forward for full-time service to fill the three-battalion quota. Instead, four divisions of companies of Incorporated Militia had been raised, these being at Prescott (six companies), Kingston (three companies), York (one company), and on the Niagara (three companies). Each of these divisions had already seen significant active service during 1813 (for additional details on this unit see author's *Redcoated Ploughboys*), but without the numbers to justify the establishment of three battalions, Drummond decided to amalgamate the divisions into a single battalion force. Under normal conditions, the geographic and military supply hub at Kingston would have been the natural location to gather these units for training and equipping. However, as there was already a strong garrison of regular troops stationed at Kingston, while that of York (Toronto) was still under-strength, Drummond decided to unify the separate units at York — there to be combined into the Volunteer Battalion of Incorporated Militia of Upper Canada and placed under the command of Captain William Robinson (8th [King's] Regiment). Lieutenant General Drummond also amended the Upper Canada Militia Acts to establish a rotating conscription within the part-time embodied militia regiments, whereby a selected number of men were drafted for three months of intensive training within the ranks of the Incorporated Militia. By these measures he hoped to improve the overall standard of the militias so they could bolster the line when needed.

During this same period, at Kingston, Commodore Sir James Yeo was having challenges of his own in the planning of his new campaign for the Lakes, once the sailing season recommenced.

- His current fleet of Lake Ontario vessels was ice-bound at Kingston and were universally in need of extensive refits and repairs from their hard service during 1813.
- While General Wilkinson's attack toward Montreal the previous autumn (for details see *The Flames of War*) had been thwarted, the growing scale of the war meant that the single main-supply lifeline of the St. Lawrence River would be even more vital to the British war effort and, in the event of an American resurgence, vulnerable to attack. Consequently, in addition to the existing land-based garrisons, Yeo determined that an enlarged gunboat fleet was required to guard this waterway and the convoys coming up from Lower Canada.
- The existing stocks of cut and prepared timber, fabricated ship fittings, sail canvas, ropes, blocks, and every other conceivable item necessary to outfit and maintain the existing vessels were either in short supply or entirely exhausted, leaving the official repair and preparation schedule in tatters.
- His roster of experienced sailors was barely

enough to properly crew his existing fleet, let alone that of any new boats that were to be launched.

- The humiliating and strategically devastating loss of the Lake Erie fleet and the strategic imperative to regain some kind of British naval presence on the upper lakes meant that he had to seriously consider directing considerable resources and manpower away from his own reserves and (more importantly to Yeo) his direct personal control.

Beyond and above these issues was the fact that Yeo was receiving increasing numbers of reports from British agents and American deserters that the Americans were preparing a new intensive program of warship construction at Sackets Harbor. If these proved true, then by the spring the Americans would emerge with a fleet of much bigger and heavier-armed vessels that could wrest control of the essential water supply lines from Yeo's smaller fleet, thus allowing them to simultaneously dominate Lake Erie, Lake Ontario, and the St. Lawrence River for the foreseeable future, possibly forcing the British to abandon Upper Canada entirely.

Believing this new shipbuilding threat to be paramount, and despite the severe challenges and costs involved, Yeo felt he had no alternative but to enter into an arms race with his American

Library and Archives Canada, C-010926.

Commodore Isaac Chauncey (U.S. naval commander, Northern frontier).

counterpart, Commodore Isaac Chauncey. To this end, not only did he have to design and build new warships in an impossibly short period of time, but these vessels needed to be big enough and sufficiently well-armed and crewed to compete with anything Chauncey could put into the water.

Fortunately, because Yeo's superiors (Sir George Prevost at Quebec and Lord Bathurst in England) concurred in the need to dominate the entire Great Lakes system, Yeo was basically given a blank cheque to get the job done to control Lake Ontario. As a result, during the winter of 1813–14, Kingston became a beehive of activity. Every available local skilled tradesman was hired and set to work in an attempt to get the first batch of vessels, consisting of two frigates and four gunboats, ready for action as soon as the ice broke up. However, when this local labour force proved inadequate to the size of the task, additional workers were recruited and taken from the Niagara and York (Toronto) areas, to the detriment of their own project timetables. In addition, experienced shipworkers were brought up from Lower Canada and even the Maritimes to ensure the work got done in time. Beyond this, an entire infrastructure of workshops and warehouses were built to either fabricate, repair, or store the necessary parts and supplies that would be needed to complete the fleet for action.

Indents for supplies to be forwarded from Lower Canada now went out by the dozens instead of singly, and supplies were requested in quantities of tons and hundreds instead of pounds and dozens. Within weeks the return shipments started to arrive in convoys of sleighs, as the St. Lawrence River remained frozen. Similarly, transfer requisitions for ships' fittings and crews were responded to by the stripping of auxiliary naval transport vessels and even warships docked on the east coast, and their subsequent overland transportation to Kingston — along with a battalion of Royal Marines and, a relatively new military novelty, a battery of Royal Marine Artillery (Congreve Rocket) troops. As a result, the Kingston waterfront at Point Frederick turned into a naval-personnel hub and ship-production centre, the likes of which had never before been seen in British North America, away from the traditional ports of Halifax and Quebec City. While the result of these

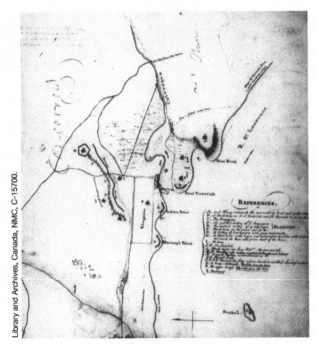

An 1814 map showing the defences of Kingston.

(Above) A view from the heights of Point Henry. Showing Fort Henry (left), the shipyards at Point Frederick (centre), and the town of Kingston (right distant) as they looked at the end of the war.

(Below) The same perspective in 2013.

efforts soon began to rise in the form of buildings around the point and on the slipways in the shapes of two frigates, subsequently to be named the *Princess Charlotte* and *Prince Regent*, and three large gunboats *Crysler*, *Queenston*, and *Niagara*.

By February, with the current warships almost complete and awaiting launching in April, Yeo took the next step in his arms race by giving orders that as soon as the slipways were clear, a new behemoth warship, the largest yet to be built outside of the British yards, was to be immediately begun and completed with maximum speed. Subsequently named the *St. Lawrence*, this vessel was to be built with no less than three full gun decks, mounting a formidable 104 guns and allowing for the reduced requirements for the displacement and draft dimensions of a lake vessel as opposed to an ocean-going one, could be roughly compared in size to the immortal *Victory* of Lord Nelson fame. Unfortunately it also proved to be a black hole of a project that gobbled up valuable resources that could have been used to readily outfit and maintain the remainder of the fleet, as well as send vital supplies up to the troops fighting on the Niagara frontier.

As if this was not enough, across the Atlantic Yeo's superiors at the Admiralty shook off their previous lethargies about the status of the Great

Metro Toronto Reference Library, JRR-1186.

HMS *St. Lawrence*. A later, unknown artist's depiction of Sir James Yeo's answer to the growing American naval threat at Sackets Harbor.

Lakes and began to actively plan for the development of a real North American fresh-water navy for the lakes. To this end, as well as sending vastly increased volumes of supplies and manpower to the region, they also looked at ways in which they could speed up the rate of production and completion of new warships entering service. For this, they took the extraordinary decision to design, develop, fabricate, and assemble the main frames and hull parts for two frigates (*Prompte* and *Psyche*) and two brigs (*Goshawk* and *Calibri*) — in kit form at the shipyards at Chatham, England! Following which, the "frigates in frame" would be transported across the ocean to Quebec or Montreal, hauled overland past the Lachine Rapids, and then brought up the St. Lawrence to Kingston for reconstruction on the Point Frederick slipways, before being planked, decked, masted, and sparred with locally provided materials and "fitted-out" with either entirely new materials or fittings stripped off vessels in port at Quebec. By then the ships would have travelled a total distance of over 4,000 miles (6,437 kilometers)! They also drafted movement and transfer orders for almost a thousand additional seamen, which were to be implemented once the prefabricated ships were delivered and well under construction.

As the total number of existing and new vessels intended for the Great Lakes would effectively double the fleet that would come under Yeo's command, their lordships also decided that the current arrangement (whereby Yeo and his fleet were linked to the army's quartermaster general's department and therefore directly under Sir George Prevost's direction) should be amended. Consequently, in January 1814, the Admiralty established an independent naval command for Yeo to oversee. His title was elevated from "Senior Officer on the Lakes" to "Commander-in-Chief of his Majesty's Ships and Vessels Employed on the Lakes," while his jurisdiction not only covered the Great Lakes and Lake Champlain, but all the intervening waterways and rivers between — as well as all of the Royal Navy and associated or linked civilian shore establishments in Upper and parts of Lower Canada. In addition, as this new command would be a distinctly Royal Navy affair, it was recognized that the existing names applied to the lakes fleet sometimes duplicated those of other pre-existing vessels already on the navy's list of vessels. Consequently, the admiralty, in its

BRITISH LAKE ONTARIO FLEET, OFFICIAL NAME CHANGES 1814[6]

Earl of Moria (ship-rigged sloop-of-war, built in 1805) becomes HMS *Charwell*

Royal George (ship-rigged sloop-of war, built in 1809) becomes HMS *Niagara*

Prince Regent (armed schooner, built in 1812 and previously renamed *Lord Beresford* in 1813) becomes HMS *Netley*

Sir George Prevost (ship-rigged sloop-of-war, built in 1813 and previously renamed *Wolfe* in 1813), becomes HMS *Montreal*

Lord Melville (brig-rigged sloop-of-war, built in 1813) becomes HMS *Star*

Sir Sydney Smith (armed schooner, built in 1808 and previously named *Governor Simcoe*) becomes HMS *Magnet*

bureaucratic wisdom, unilaterally reclassified and renamed Yeo's ships to avoid official confusion.*6

Thus, in a single stroke of the pen, Sir George Prevost no longer had a direct subordinate under his command or control over the Lake Ontario fleet, but a separate naval establishment and independent associate commander with whom he was now expected to co-operate and coordinate the future campaigns of the war in Upper Canada — a fact that obviously did not sit well with Sir George. In a sop to Prevost's pride and in an attempt to cut off any future argument, Lord Bathurst wrote to Prevost on January 20, 1814.

> It has been determined ... to extend the scale of Naval exertions; and feeling that to impose on you the conduct of Naval operations so much more extended than heretofore, would be to increase unnecessarily the responsibility of your situation, I have thought it best ... to submit to the Lords Commissioners of the Admiralty, the necessity of taking charge of all the Naval establishment on the lakes, and placing the fleets and dock yards there on a similar footing with His Majesty's fleets and dock yards in other parts of the world.[7]

Unfortunately, this communication did not have its desired effect, as Prevost's pride was distinctly hurt, resulting in a soured working relationship between Prevost and Yeo once the two commanders' divergent opinions on how the campaigns should be conducted and respective jurisdictions of authority came into conflict. As an aside to this British naval segment, it should also be noted that at the end of February 1814 the detachment of naval personnel previously sent up from Kingston to participate in the now-cancelled Lake Erie operation were diverted north with new orders to travel overland to Georgian Bay and commence the establishment of a small gunboat dockyard facility in a naturally sheltered anchorage on the Penetanguishene inlet. However, once they finally arrived, the detachment, under the command of Lieutenant Newdigate Poyntz, R.N., found the undeveloped shoreline and rocky terrain made their assigned task almost impossible without considerably more manpower and resources. Consequently, they relocated further round Georgian Bay into the Nottawasaga River (at today's Wasaga Beach), where the vastly better low and sandy ground permitted the groundbreaking for boat construction.

Meanwhile, during this same period and south of the border at Sackets Harbor, Commodore Isaac Chauncey had ended the 1813 shipping season by

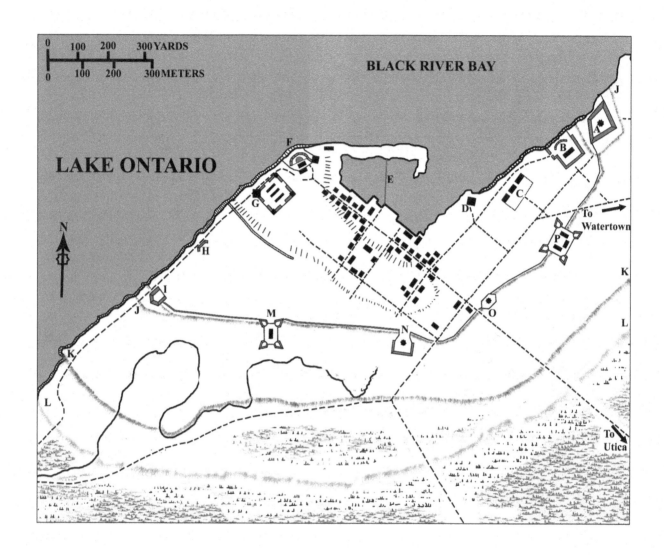

SACKETS HARBOUR DEFENCES, SPRING 1814

A   Fort Pike (built partially on the site of the former Fort Volunteer)

B   Pike Cantonment (comprising rebuilt elements of Fort Volunteer with an artillery position)

C   Madison Barracks

D   Blockhouse

E   Floating pontoon bridge, connecting the dockyard to the cleared Navy Point

F   Rebuilt and enlarged Fort Tompkins

G   Smith Fortified Encampment

H   Artillery battery and execution gallows

I   Fort Mud (later renamed Fort Kentucky)

JJ   Line of new perimeter defences, consisting of earthworks (connecting Fort Kentucky to Fort Virginia), picket fencing (connecting Fort Virginia to Fort Pike), and abattis (connecting all positions from Fort Kentucky to Fort Pike), running approximately along the line of the former inner line of abattis

KK   Repaired and strengthened line of abattis (approximately along the line of the former middle line of abattis)

LL   Former outer line of abattis (constructed February 1813, derelict and overgrown)

M   Stone magazine fortification

N   Fort Virginia

O   Fort Chauncey

P   Fort Stark

immediately beginning work on his own plans and strategies for how he would conduct his 1814 naval campaign. His main shipbuilding base had been attacked and almost overwhelmed by the British the previous May, and had only survived by good luck and the premature withdrawal of those forces by the British commander on that day, Sir George Prevost (for details see *The Pendulum of War*). With several of his warehouses and workshops already either destroyed or damaged (by the self-inflicted fire that had been set by the retreating American forces as part of the battle), Chauncey decided to wipe the slate clean around the harbour and erect a new infrastructure for the repair of his existing fleet (which was in a desperate need of refitting), and the construction of a number of new vessels to replace those deemed too deteriorated to be worth salvaging. To this end, Chauncey set his dockyard workforce to the task of clearing the required ground, while his associate, Master Commandant William Crane, used his regular and militia troops to begin the overhaul and revamping of the land-based fortifications and defences that were supposed to stop another landing and overland attack by the British. Chauncey also petitioned Secretary of War Armstrong for the transfer of sufficient additional regular troops from their winter quarters at French Mills to properly man these new defences.

After reviewing the state of his available vessels, Chauncey ordered the worst-state vessels (*Conquest*, *Fair American*, *Pert*, and *Julia*) to be taken out of commission and scavenged for parts, while their crews were consolidated into those of the more seaworthy *Sylph*, *Madison*, and *General Pike*. What is important to note, however, is that as late as December 1813 nothing was actually being built by way of new warships in Sackets Harbor, nor were there any approvals forthcoming from the Washington administration for such a program, or shipbuilding supplies of any quantity on hand, even if there had been an approval. Nonetheless, the clearance work that was undertaken was sufficient to cause Yeo to begin his shipbuilding race. And if there were spies and informers for the British in Sackets Harbor, it was nothing compared to the American spies in Kingston. Consequently, Chauncey soon learned of Yeo's building program. Determined not to be outdone and see his fleet outgunned and overmatched, Chauncey immediately contacted the secretary of the navy, William Jones, to approve a new shipbuilding program that would see an enlarged and improved fleet ready to take on Yeo in the spring. Once this approval arrived (on December 23, 1813), the floodgates were opened and Sackets Harbour became a mirror image of Kingston, as skilled tradesmen, raw and finished timbers, ships fittings, ships crews, armaments, and every other imaginable requirement were ordered up to that pre-war isolated and insignificant village. By January, the hulls of two brigs and a large frigate were already laid down on the new slipways and the dockside workshops were running around the clock to catch up with the already implemented British shipbuilding program.

Unfortunately, an unusually bad period of frigid local temperatures, coupled with blizzards and rainstorms across the eastern seaboard and Appalachian Mountains, effectively rendered the roads leading to Sackets Harbor impassable quagmires, thus delaying and impeding numerous shipments of vitally needed supplies and imperilling the construction timetables. In addition, the huge construction upheaval and massive influx of dockyard personnel (estimated at over 2,500) completely swamped the existing infrastructure of sanitation and sewage disposal within the complex. As a result, with the creeks and harbour frozen over and currents impeded, the accumulation of human effluent, combined with the detritus from animal slaughtering and food preparation, became so overpowering that sickness inevitably began to soar. By February the death rate was so high that the daily issuance of public notices and the playing of appropriate music at military funerals were suspended so as not to alarm the local population or reduce the already low morale of the troops.

In another parallel to Yeo's plans at Kingston, Commodore Chauncey looked to raise the ante on the arms race by proposing that as soon as the new vessels were launched, work should commence on a new super-frigate that would dominate and outgun anything Yeo could produce. To further his cause, Chauncey left Sackets Harbor and journeyed to

(Above) *South East View of Sackets Harbor.*

(Below) The same view in 2012.

Washington to personally meet with sympathetic politicians and the secretary of the navy, William Jones. Once there, however, he found the American war administration was in a state of shambles, with political infighting and accusations of corruption and malfeasance topping the agenda of the senior American cabinet.

For example, the secretary of war, John Armstrong, held that a massive increase in the size of the army and navy were essential if the war on the

Northern frontier was to be prosecuted successfully, and was making bold promises to pro-war Republicans in New York State of a winter campaign to recapture Fort Niagara from the British. On the other hand, Secretary of State James Monroe and Secretary of the Navy William Jones were favouring the adoption of proposals that had just arrived from the British government for the establishment of negotiations to produce a peace treaty. They were also openly blaming Armstrong for General Wilkinson's failed invasion against Montreal the previous November (for details see *The Flames of War*) and were demanding Armstrong's impeachment and dismissal on the grounds of his constant interference in the planning and implementation of that operation.

Caught in the middle, President James Madison was forced to both veto Armstrong's planned Fort Niagara campaign and then support him by denying Monroe and Jones his removal from office. In addition, while Chauncey was looking for a huge outlay of funding to undertake his new building program, he found that the U.S. finances were in a state of crisis, as the war debt had spiralled out of control during the 1812 and 1813 campaigns, leaving the country close to fiscal bankruptcy. The newly appointed treasury administrator, Senator George Campbell, had also just dropped the bombshell that on top of the current war debt the already

established budget for war expenditures in 1814 would exceed thirty million dollars and there was virtually no reserve or income from which it could be paid. This situation was partially Madison's own fault, as since 1808 a series of domestically detested government legislations, commonly referred to as the *Embargo* and *Non-Intercourse Bills*, had not only interfered with American shipping and trade with Europe, but also eliminated most of the lucrative duties and taxes that had previously been the main source of American public funding (for details see *The Call to Arms*). Desperate to refill the nation's coffers, Madison was now being forced into the contradictory position of advocating the adoption of legislation that would repeal the "embargo" in order to reopen and encourage trade with Europe — including Great Britain — while still fighting a war against her in British North America.

Madison also had to contend with the irrefutable fact that the favourable foreign conditions that had existed at the time of the declaration of war (namely that of Britain being fully involved with fighting what had appeared to be an unwinnable war against Napoleon Bonaparte) had now turned into a distinct likelihood that Napoleon and his empire were about to fall, potentially releasing Britain's military machine for use against the United States. He had therefore played for time and a negotiating edge (through campaign victories by his military) by agreeing to send a delegation to Europe to begin negotiations for peace. However, upon reaching Europe the discussions could not even begin, as the two countries could not agree upon a location for these talks. The U.S. contingent therefore initially went to St. Petersburg, before transferring to London, England, and Gotheburg, Sweden, before ending up in Ghent in Belgium later in the year. In addition, once discussions began, the American delegation was supplemented by the addition of hard-line "War Hawks" and the least likely to offer or agree to any conciliatory concessions on the part of the Americans.

Despite all these issues, Chauncey got his way, and returned to Sackets Harbor in late February to find his new ships well on the way to completion and carrying the approvals for the start of not one but two super-frigates, as soon as the slipways were available.

In counterpart to the resurgence of the American naval efforts at Sackets Harbor, the entire American land forces were in the midst of a crisis affecting the very continuance of a standing army. Originally planned on paper to consist of over 58,000 troops, the American army had never topped 30,000 fit for duty during the course of the conflict thus far. In addition, while the muster rolls in January 1814 showed a force of 26,714 enlisted men, the actual duty strength was calculated at less than half that number. Furthermore, this number was about to be decimated as a result of the calendar and a contractual technicality. This circumstance had arisen because many of the currently serving troops had originally signed up for a five-year term of enlistment during the war scare of 1808 and 1809. This term of service was now ending and would soon release thousands of men from their military obligations. Similarly, the eighteen-month term soldiers who joined at the commencement of the war and twelve-month enlistees from 1813 were reaching the end of their requirements. In response, Congress was forced to pass an additional emergency financial bill boosting the (re) enlistment bounty to a staggering $124.00 per man, accompanied by a promised post-war grant of 320 acres of free land, in order to persuade the majority of the current soldiers to re-enlist and to attract new recruits.

At the same time, on the Northern frontier the remnants of Wilkinson's army remained singularly inactive following the collapse of their campaign against Montreal. Abandoned by most of their senior and even mid-rank officers (who either took furloughs or claimed urgent business elsewhere), the rank and file were left without leadership, supplies of clothing, food, or even firewood in their singularly unhealthy and isolated winter quarters at French Mills. However, at the beginning of February 1814 the situation began to change when Brigadier General Jacob Brown was ordered to make a forced march west to Sackets Harbor with two thousand men, while Major General Wilkinson was sent back to French Mills with orders to march the bulk of the remaining troops to the east and place them in better winter quarters around Plattsburg on Lake Champlain.

Unfortunately, Wilkinson, still smarting from his failure on the St. Lawrence and the vitriolic criticism that was circulating against him, decided against simply relocating to Plattsburg, rebuilding his forces, and commencing spring operations in accordance with future directives from Washington. Instead, he mounted an attack into Lower Canada in late March at the head of some 4,000 troops — only

Major General Jacob Brown, attributed to J. Wood, engraver.

Major General James Wilkinson.

to have his troops flounder about in heavy drifts of snow and quagmires of mud, before making an abortive attack on a negligible and isolated outpost of Canadian militia at Lacolle Mills. Unable to sweep aside even this paltry opposition, Wilkinson's new invasion attempt collapsed and the entire column turned and retreated to the United States under a cloud of humiliation and shame.

Wilkinson's removal from command seemed inevitable. However, unwilling to pre-empt such a humiliation by resigning, Wilkinson chose instead to demand a court of inquiry about his actions. Initially, Armstrong and the administration agreed, concluding that it would be a foregone conclusion and of no consequence how Wilkinson was removed from command, as long as he was gone. Once details started emerging about the embarrassing and incriminating testimonies that would be presented, however, their minds quickly changed and the proposed court of inquiry was just as quickly shelved, so as to avoid any revelations that could lead to the public embarrassment of government officials. Instead, Major General Wilkinson was informed that the inquiry would be suspended as subsequent events "… make it imprudent to go on as intended with an investigation into your military conduct at present…. You will choose between Philadelphia, Baltimore, or Annapolis as a place of residence. Report your arrival and await further orders."[8]

Finally, and by no coincidence, there followed the transfer of Major General Morgan Lewis and Brigadier General John Boyd (two of the other principal players in the St. Lawrence debacle) to positions where they no longer had a part to play in the upcoming campaigns or were likely to cause trouble. Replacing these relative failures, Brigadier Generals Jacob Brown and George Izard were promoted to major general, while several regimental commanders were raised to the rank of brigadier general, including: David Bissell, Edmund Gaines, Alexander Macomb, Eleazer Ripley, Winfield Scott, and Joseph Swift.

Thus the various contenders and foes were each dealt the new hands with which they were expected to contend with for the control of the Northern frontier.

CHAPTER 3

The Winter of Discontent in the West

During this same period, in the western reaches of Upper Canada, the war continued unabated. This was because despite the American victories at the battles of Lake Erie (September 10, 1813) and the Thames/Moravianstown (October 5, 1813), the subsequent British victories at Crysler's Farm (November 11, 1813) and on the Niagara frontier (December 1813) meant that neither side had enough "disposable" resources to establish a lasting firm control of this relatively distant region in western Upper Canada.

For the British, having lost control of the Detroit frontier, their new western line of defensive outposts were strategically placed to give the maximum "early warning" of any American incursions, running in a wide arc from Port Dover, Long Point, and Port Talbot, northerly to Delaware and then back northeast to Oxford (Beamsville-Ingersoll). Officially garrisoned by a rotating cadre of local militia detachments, additional "stiffening" was provided by companies of regular troops, who were periodically moved from location to location to give the impression of having a larger number of troops within the region. For the Americans, the Detroit River remained its principal front line, with temporary or isolated advance posts being established at sympathetic farmsteads along the Thames River and along the Talbot Road, leading from Amherstburg toward Long Point.

As a result, the region between became an effective no man's land during the winter of 1813–14. That is not to say that this part of Upper Canada became peaceful. Far from it, in fact, as both sides sent reconnaissance, raiding, and supply gathering

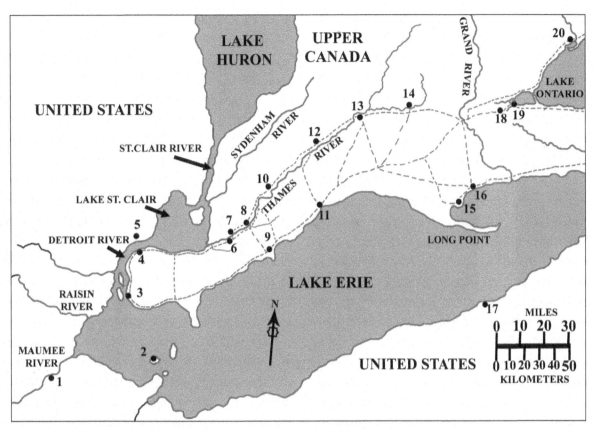

The Detroit Frontier in 1814

1. Perrysburg [Fort Meigs]
2. Put-in-Bay
3. Amherstburg [Fort Malden]
4. Sandwich (Windsor)
5. Detroit
6. Thomas McCrea's Farmstead
7. Dolsen's Farmstead
8. Forks of the Thames (Chatham)
9. Rondeau
10. Moravianstown
11. Port Talbot
12. Battle of the Longwoods
13. Delaware
14. Oxford (Ingersoll-Beachville)
15. Long Point
16. Dover (Port Dover)
17. Presque Isle (Erie, PA)
18. Ancaster
19. Burlington Heights
20. York (Toronto) [Fort York]

parties throughout the region in an attempt to elicit information and supplies for their own side while disrupting and harassing the enemy on the other. In addition, while the bulk of the western Native allies had either evacuated into the Burlington Heights defensive enclave or abandoned the British altogether, small bands of western warriors continued to wage guerrilla-style warfare behind the American "front line," while being supplied with arms and ammunition by the British from their forward bases. Inevitably, detachments from all sides would occasionally come across each other and clash in brief but deadly skirmishes that ranged from a few dozen to a few hundred men in total.

While most of these engagements remain only scantily recorded, some events are more fully described. These include the clash that took place on November 13, 1813, known as the fight at Nanticoke Creek. This engagement began when a party of Upper-Canadian American sympathizers, who had previously joined the renegade regiment known as the "Canadian Volunteers," participated in a series of American attacks upon the settlements located along the Lake Erie shoreline, looting considerable amounts of booty and supplies before beginning their journey back to their base at Buffalo. In response, a detachment of around fifty men, drawn from the 1st and 2nd Norfolk County Embodied Militia regiments and Oxford County Embodied Militia Regiment, set out in pursuit and retaliation. Tracking the culprits through the bush, they captured two of the enemy pickets and extorted the required information about the location and dispositions of the remainder of the enemy's force. Approaching the cabin in which the enemy renegades were supposed to be sleeping, the militiamen divided into two parties, covering the front and rear to prevent the enemy's escape. When no alarm was raised, and confident of their success, two of the Canadian officers, Lieutenant John Bostwick (1st Norfolk) and Lieutenant Jonathan Austin (2nd Norfolk), approached the cabin and pushed their luck too far by opening the cabin door, only to come face to face with a roomful of awake, alert, and armed Canadian Volunteers. Rapidly adopting a bold bluster, the two officers strode inside and demanded the renegades immediate surrender, claiming the cabin was surrounded by a vastly superior number of troops. Some of the enemy party began to comply, but when no additional loyal militia troops appeared to support Bostwick and Austin the renegades' fear evaporated and they again grabbed their weapons before attempting to disarm the Upper-Canadian militia officers. In the ensuing scuffle, weapons were discharged, wounding Bostwick and one of the renegades. It also alerted the surrounding militiamen that the surprise had failed, causing them to rush toward the cabin, firing as they went. In reply, the "volunteers" fired back, driving off the initial charge. During the following exchange of gunfire, Bostwick and Austin were trapped inside the cabin and rapidly took cover to avoid both enemy and friendly fire. As casualties mounted within the building, some of the renegades attempted to break out of their trap by making a run for the woods. Three were killed and at least two wounded and captured, while a possible half dozen, including their leader Benajah Mallory, succeeded in escaping. Abandoned by Mallory, the remaining seventeen men inside the building immediately surrendered to the Canadian officers. However, as renegade Canadian settlers fighting on the side of the enemy, these men could expect little mercy and were thereafter placed in close confinement at York, pending the finding of trials upon the charge of treason — trials that did not take place for several months.

A further incident occurred in December, when a detachment of a dozen men from the 2nd Norfolk County Embodied Militia and seven from the Provincial Light Dragoons, all under the command of Lieutenant Henry Medcalf, were ordered to march the sixty-five miles (105 kilometers) from Dover Mills to Port Talbot. Once there, they were to scour the surrounding country for cattle being wintered in this fertile spot to deny them being taken by an American raiding party reported to be somewhere in the vicinity. Arriving at Port Talbot, Lieutenant Medcalf's detachment was joined by nine men from the Middlesex County Embodied Militia (Lieutenant Moses Rice), who had more definite intelligence of the Americans' whereabouts and numbers. Learning that the reported raiding party consisted of around forty American regular troops from the Twenty-Sixth Regiment, under the command of a Lieutenant Larwell, Medcalf also learned that this force was reputed to be headquartered at a known American sympathiser's (Thomas McCrea's) farm, some sixty miles (97 kilometers) away and within only eight miles (13 kilometers) of the mouth of the River Thames. Nonetheless, Medcalf decided on making the daring and decidedly difficult attempt to mount a surprise attack on the enemy, and to do it without any regular troops in support.

Advancing throughout the night and following day in a non-stop march across the frozen and snow-covered countryside, Medcalf's small strike force was further enhanced en route by the addition of seven men of the Loyal Kent Volunteers (Lieutenant John McGregor). Reaching the locality of McCrea's farmstead without being detected on the night of December 14/15, McCrea was then forced to leave some men behind due to their extreme exhaustion caused by the forced march. Just before dawn the remaining troops, totalling thirty-one men, took up positions in an arc around the farmstead with orders not to fire until ordered. Fortunately, the Americans had posted no sentries and the entire body of the enemy were inside as dawn arrived. Seizing the advantage of the moment, Medcalf called out, demanding the Americans' surrender. In reply, shouts of alarm could be heard from within the house, followed quickly by a series of shots from the windows. Returning fire, the Canadian militiamen quickly proved the truth of their strategic advantage by shooting out the windows of the farmhouse. Shortly thereafter, a white flag was waved from the doorway and the American force of three officers and thirty-five other ranks surrendered, having suffered five wounded in the engagement.

Because of the threat of American reinforcements arriving at any moment, Medcalf ordered an immediate retreat to his own lines, while putting the American wounded (one of whom shortly thereafter died of his wounds) in the care of Thomas McCrea. Marching his captives back to Port Dover without suffering a single casualty, Medcalf and his small detachment had the distinction of having travelled overland, through the Canadian bush, in the depths of winter, a distance of no less than 250 miles (402 kilometers) in less than a week. In addition, this small capture remained the only recorded instance during the course of the war of a Canadian militia unit single-handedly capturing a regular U.S. army unit.

After this alarming nearby event, the Americans re-garrisoned the McCrea position with no less than two hundred troops and imposed oaths of future neutrality and non-aggression upon the local population — using threats of retaliation in the form of the destruction of property and the arrest, imprisonment, and possible execution of anyone suspected of assisting the British.

While these minor victories did promote pride and boost morale within Upper Canada, the increased levels of American aggression and reprisals led the British to also reinforce their outposts with additional detachments of regular troops to supplement the local militias. Unfortunately, these regular soldiers had no particular affinity or investment in the isolated and remote locations wherein they had been "dumped." As a result, discontent and boredom sometimes led these supposed defenders to act in a manner more reminiscent of the enemy, creating a deep rift between themselves and the local communities and the militiamen they served alongside.

I propose posting [the 100th Regiment] … in the vicinity of Mr Culver's house … from whence a small party may be detached to Oxford … Turkey Point,

Mrs Ryerson's and Dover ... as that part of this corps, stationed there before ... conducted itself, collectively and individually, in the most orderly and correct manner during its service there. Very widely different, I am forced to say, from the light companies of the Royals [1st (Royal Scots)] and 89th regiments, whose behaviour has been more of a plundering banditti than of British soldiers employed for the protection of the country and its inhabitants.[1]

— Drummond to Prevost,
March 5, 1814

However, not all engagements between the two sides favoured the British/Canadian allies. For example, in late January a composite detachment of over seventy men, drawn from the 1st Middlesex County Embodied Militia, the Oxford Rifles, and the 1st Kent County Embodied Militia were garrisoned at Delaware on the Thames River. Occupying local homes, the detachments were well ensconced, but their relative isolation and the winter weather led to an increasing laxity in alertness and attention to duty. As a result, a former prominent resident of Delaware and American sympathizer, Andrew Westbrook (who had previously abandoned his home and family to fight with the Americans), was able to lead a strong raiding party (drawn from the Michigan Rangers militia regiment) undetected through the surrounding countryside. On the night of January 31st/February 1st, 1814, the Americans crossed the frozen Thames River before descending on the badly defended settlement. With a full knowledge of the locations of the Canadian militia officers and their detachments, Westbrook and his American cohorts were able to overrun the defenders without significant opposition, catching most in bed asleep. Paroling the rank and file, Westbrook opted to take into captivity the principal Canadian militia officers, Captain Daniel Springer (1st Middlesex), Lieutenant Colonel Francois Baby (2nd Essex), Captain Belah B. Brigham (1st Oxford, Rifle Company), and Lieutenant John Dolsen (1st Kent). He also collected his family and as many possessions as could be transported in sleighs, before setting fire to his remaining possessions, buildings, and their contents and retreating to Detroit — while his American associates raided additional nearby barns and houses to appropriate loot and provisions for their own return trip.

In a direct response to this raid, Lieutenant George Jackson (1st [Royal Scots] Regiment) was dispatched with an official delegation to Detroit under a flag of truce to register a formal complaint for the "abduction" of the Canadian militia officers and the looting of private properties. In response, the Detroit commander, Lieutenant Colonel Butler, not only dismissed these complaints, but as he had two additional intelligence and supply gathering raids still on patrol in Upper Canada, he detained the British delegation for a number of days until both raiding parties returned to the American side of the river.

The first of these parties consisted of a combined detachment of Michigan Rangers (Captain William Gill) and Michigan Militia Dragoons (Captain Lee) numbering between eighty and a hundred men. This force had left Detroit on February 22nd with orders to forage and reconnoitre along the Thames River Valley before uniting with the second foraging detachment at a pre-arranged rendezvous point at Rondeau (southeast of the Forks of the Thames [Chatham]). Stripping the farms they passed of their livestock, grain, and anything else that came to hand, the raiders received intelligence that a detachment of Kent County Embodied Militia had been alerted to their presence and were actively on patrol. Seeking to avoid the enemy, Captain Gill moved south from the Thames Valley, toward the designated rendezvous point.

During this same period, the second, larger, raiding party had been advancing along the Talbot Road and Lake Erie shoreline under Captain Andrew Hunter Holmes, the commandant of the newly constructed American defensive fortification at Amherstburg, Fort Malden. This column had exhibited much the same behaviour as Gills' force in forcibly "acquiring" supplies, while also being charged with the duty of making raids on the British advance post at Port Talbot. However, due to a temporary and sudden thaw in the weather, the previously firm ground had degenerated into a heavy mud that slowed the infantry and cavalry to a crawl, but entirely bogged down the heavier artillery pieces and supply wagons until it became obvious that no further advance would be possible if they remained with the column. Equally unable to retreat back to Amherstburg on their own, it was decided to temporarily abandon the guns and associated wagons in a secreted location and proceed with the rest of the mission before returning to reclaim these valuable pieces on the return leg of the journey. In addition, during their advance, Holmes' force had captured a small group of Canadian militiamen who were travelling toward Port Talbot to rejoin their regiment. However, two of these prisoners (John Fulmer/Fuller and Alexander Wilkinson) were able to escape and fled toward Port Talbot to raise the alarm.

Linking up with Gill's force, Holmes and Gill held a council of officers that came to the conclusion that as the British had, by now, been fully alerted by the escaped prisoners, and would expect an attack on Port Talbot, the best option for the

American combined force was to double back to Gill's route and attack the British advance position at Delaware.

THE BATTLE OF THE LONGWOODS, MARCH 4, 1814

The combined American force, numbering between 180 and 200 all ranks, moved north from their rendezvous back into the Thames River Valley, picking up the main road paralleling the river at the destroyed ruins of Moravianstown (Fairfield). Turning east, they marched under weather conditions that had once again turned icy cold, accompanied by blinding snow squalls. With his men showing increasing signs of exhaustion and exposure, Holmes ordered a halt some twenty miles (32 kilometers) short of Delaware, at a point where the road dropped down into a small but steep-sided ravine on what was referred to as the Twenty-Mile Creek. On the west side of this natural obstacle, the Americans cut down timber and brushwood to erect a chest-high rectangular defensive enclave on the rear and two flanks of their new camp's perimeter, while the natural obstacle of the steep slope of the ravine, topped by a lesser wall of abattis, was considered sufficient to defend the front face.

On the morning of March 3rd, the column had advanced a further fifteen miles (24 kilometers), when they intercepted a local settler and militiaman, George Ward (1st Kent Militia). Stripping the over seventy-year-old man to his underclothes in the frigid air, they eventually succeeded in extorting information from him that the Delaware garrison was not only composed of substantial numbers of militia but two companies of newly arrived regulars from the 1st (Royal Scots) and 89th regiments, numbering over 300 troops in all, almost double that of the American force.

Seeking to verify this intelligence, Holmes detached an advance force to reconnoitre the road ahead, only to have it run into Ward's company of Kent militia. Following an exchange of gunfire, the Americans withdrew and reported back to Holmes. The element of surprise had now been lost, and with the prospect of facing a greatly superior number of enemy troops, not to mention the fact that a large proportion of them were regulars, Holmes ordered a wholesale retreat to their camp at the ravine — not knowing that he and his force were already under a hidden watch by men of Captain William Caldwell's "Western Rangers," most of whom, interestingly, are recorded as being black, or in the terms of the time "men of colour." At the same time, at Delaware, the senior officer in command of the London District, Captain (brevetted to

Lieutenant Colonel) Alexander Stewart of the 1st (Royal Scots) Regiment, was in the midst of dealing with a critical issue affecting his Native allies, who were still actively engaged in guerrilla activities behind the American lines. To support this, other tribes had been persuaded to act as couriers and transporters of weapons and ammunition. However, bad news had arrived from the Native agent Colonel Matthew Elliott.

Delaware, March 4th, 1814

Sir, I have this day had a meeting with the Natives on the subject of carrying ammunition to their friends within the American territory. The result is that they refuse to proceed with the ammunition on the ground that our regular troops do not advance further than the settlements on the River Thames, and of course would be of no use in protecting their friends in the enemy's country. The Americans might hear of these supplies being sent to the Natives, and the consequences would be fatal, perhaps, to their whole tribes. They would, therefore, rather suffer for want of ammunition than endanger themselves or their families.[2]

Faced with this important issue and simultaneously receiving a report from Captain Caldwell that his command had "fallen in with a party of Americans,"[3] but without providing any specifics as to their numbers or dispositions, Stewart made the critical decision to personally attend to the Native issue by holding face-to-face talks with the Native leaders, while directing his second-in-command, Captain James Basden (89th Regiment) to command a strong reconnaissance force[*4] that would advance toward the reported enemy position. Stewart would then join the force once the meetings were held and the issues resolved.

Advancing from Delaware down the Longwoods road on the morning of March 4, 1813, the

BRITISH AND ALLIED FORCES, BATTLE OF THE LONGWOODS, MARCH 4, 1814[*4]

Light Company, 1st (Royal Scots) Regiment
(Captain David Johnstone)
Light Company, 89th regiment
(Captain James Basden) (combined est. 150 rank and file)
Loyal Kent Volunteer militia
(Captain John McGregor) est. 50 rank and file
Caldwell's Western Ranger's
(Captain William Caldwell) est. 30 rank and file
Native Volunteers
(Captain "Billy" Caldwell) est. 40 warriors
Estimated Total, 300 all ranks

troops not only had to contend with the bitter cold, but also the fact that nearly a foot (30 centimeters) of new soft snow covered the previous frozen layers of snow and ice, thus creating an exhausting and treacherous surface upon which to march the twenty miles (32 kilometers) to where the enemy was reported to be still encamped.

Meanwhile, on the east bank of the Twenty Mile Creek, Captain William Caldwell and his rangers maintained their watch across the ravine and noted the American movements. An escalating skirmish soon developed between the two forces. Significantly outnumbered, and without the cover of darkness or secrecy, Caldwell's force began a rapid retreat up the Longwoods Road, leaving behind portions of their camp baggage. In response, Captain Holmes, being appraised of the relatively small enemy force involved and believing this constituted the bulk of the enemy before him, later recounted: "Mortified at the supposition of having retrograded from this diminutive force, I instantly commenced in pursuit with the intention of attacking Delaware before the opening of another day."[5]

However, Holmes' force had advanced only a matter of a few miles before the mounted advance guard returned in haste, bearing reports that a sizeable British force was directly ahead and appeared to be deploying for battle. Believing he had been deliberately tricked into leaving his strongpoint for the purpose of forcing him to fight in the open with a significant numerical disadvantage, Holmes ordered another immediate retreat. Arriving back at their encampment, some of the detachment's officers advocated a further retreat and abandonment of the entire expedition, while others called for a "victory or death" stand. Deciding to hold the position, Holmes dispatched a party of his sickest men back toward Detroit before ordering the strengthening of the breastworks against attack and deploying his limited force.[*6]

Advancing down the road from Delaware, Captain Basden linked up with Caldwell's detachment and then pressed on with his augmented

---

AMERICAN DISPOSITIONS, BATTLE OF THE LONGWOODS, MARCH 4, 1814[*6]

Front/Ravine Flank (east face)
Twenty-Fourth Tennessee Militia (Lieutenant Potter/ Lieutenant Jackson)
Twenty-Eighth Kentucky Militia (Lieutenant Knox/ Lieutenant Henry)
Left Flank (north face)
Twenty-Sixth Vermont Militia (unknown)
Twenty-Seventh New York State Militia (unknown)
Right Flank (south face)
Michigan Militia Dragoons (Captain Lee)
Rear Flank (west face)
Michigan Rangers (Captain William Gill)
Estimated total force, 160 all ranks

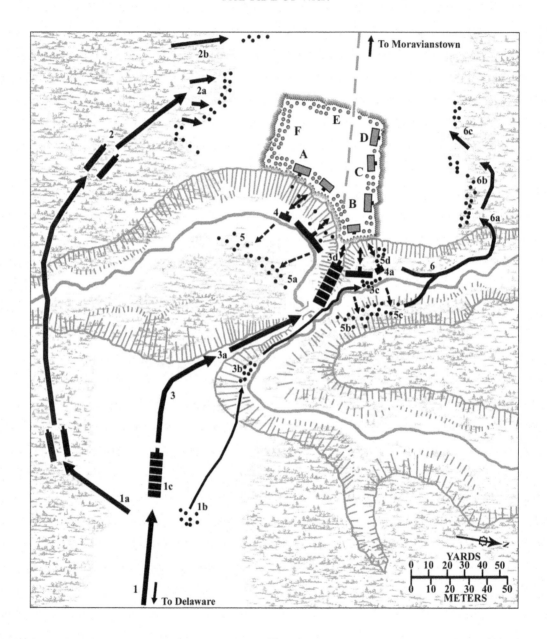

THE BATTLE OF THE LONGWOODS, MARCH 4, 1814

American Dispositions

A	Twenty-Fourth Tennessee Militia
B	Twenty-Eighth Kentucky Militia
C	Twenty-Seventh New York State Militia
D	Twenty-Sixth Vermont Militia
E	Michigan Rangers
F	Michigan Militia Dragoons

1. The British force arrives in column (1), marching down the road from Delaware. Deciding to make an immediate assault, Captain Basden detaches the Kent Militia and Caldwell's Rangers (1a) to his left, with orders to pass round the enemy's position and then signal their readiness to attack with a bugle call. He also detaches his Native allies (1b) to secure his right flank, while his main body of 1st (Royal Scots) and 89th Regiments (1c) is to advance directly along the roadway.
2. Moving through the dense bush, the Kent Militia and Caldwell's Western Rangers detachments (2) reach their assigned positions and disperse along the wood line (2a, 2b), but apart from some intermittent forays make no concerted attempt to attack the entrenched American units stationed on that flank (F, E).
3. Hearing the agreed bugle signal, Basden orders the main column forward to the attack (3). Coming under fire at the top of the ravine, the column is temporarily halted (3a) but regroups and pushes on and crosses the creek bridge, covered on its right by the augmented Native force (3b, 3c). Making their initial attacks in column (3d) directly up the slope of the road, the British assault is broken by intense American fire (A, B) and the slippery ground conditions.
4. Failing to breach the American line by column attack, the British fan out and attempt to form line. However, the broken and obstructed ground only permits a disrupted line of sections (4, 4a) to be established. Attacks are continued without success by sections and groups of individuals.
5. Unable to make any headway, the bulk of the 1st (Royal Scots), located on the left of the British position, retire and take up a dispersed firing position along the ravine (5, 5a). Similarly, most of the 89th and Native troops retire and establish a similar dispersed firing line (5b, 5c) on the right of the road, while some individuals remain on the American side of the creek and continue firing at the Americans from a point-blank range (5d).
6. Basden gathers together a force of troops and Natives (6) and attempts an outflanking manoeuvre to the right. Emerging from the ravine (6a), the flanking force finds itself facing additional defences and fresh American troops (B, C, D). Unable to make a direct assault, Basden has no alternative but to disperse his troops along the wood line (6b) and continue a harassing fire, while the detachment of Native allies (6c) move further around to complete the flanking of the American position. From these positions the engagement continues till its conclusion.

force of around 250 regulars, militia, and Native allies, reaching the vicinity of the Twenty Mile Creek in the late afternoon. As the sun was close to setting and with no sign of Lieutenant Colonel Stewart arriving to take over command and direct operations, Basden was left with the difficult options of:

- Making an immediate attack with a force of exhausted troops upon an enemy of indeterminate numbers and situated in a prepared defensive position.
- Encamping his own force within the immediate vicinity of that same enemy force and risking them making a nighttime sortie on his encampment.
- Retiring a few miles to encamp with more safety, but with the chance that his quarry would then evade his pickets and escape down the Longwoods Road under the cover of darkness.

Deciding to strike while the opportunity of proximity and daylight still existed, Basden undertook no detailed reconnaissance of the enemy dispositions before making his initial deployments. Unfortunately, in the aftermath of this action, the report made by Captain Basden was delayed by nearly a week, the result of his having been wounded. Instead, a second report, made only the day after the event by Lieutenant Colonel Stewart, became the official version of events, but contains contradictory details on the specific flanks upon which the militia and Native contingents were deployed. As a result, I have chosen to accept the report of the officer in command and on the spot for my version of events — although those who prefer Stewart's second-hand account simply need to "mirror" the flanking deployments, without changing the outcome. According to Basden's report:

> On approaching the place where the enemy had been before seen, it was observed that by the smoke and some noise that they were occupying the same ground. I therefore made my dispositions for an immediate attack, it growing late, they were posted on the opposite side of a ravine, on a high bank close to the road, and I thought I could perceive a slight brushwood fence, thrown up as I presumed to obstruct the road.[7]

Deeming this obstacle as representing only a moderate hindrance, he decided to make a direct frontal column attack with his regulars that would break through directly into the enemy's encampment. At the same time, his militia force would move round on the enemy's flank:

> The Kent Volunteers with the Rangers I directed to file through the woods to my left, and by making an extensive circle, they were to post themselves in rear of the enemy, get as near as possible, not to fire a shot, but to sound a bugle whenever the position was

properly secured and they were prepared to advance.[8]

Similarly, his Native detachment, which at this
last minute was augmented by some additional late
arrivals, was to be "stationed to flank my right, and
advance with the main body."[9] When the call was
heard, the regulars, led by an advance party from the
1st (Royal Scots) Regiment advanced down the ravine in a solid column of men, probably five to eight
men across and from twenty to thirty deep. While
this human "battering ram" had the disadvantage
of reducing the number of men who could fire at
the enemy, it had the advantage of maintaining its
solidity and inertia in an attack of this kind, and
despite taking the inevitable casualties could have
been expected to punch its way through a relatively
thin line of opposing troops, especially that of militia, thus breaking the American formation. What
Basden had not taken into consideration was that,
in addition to the enemy's troops formed directly
along the top of the ravine, there were additional
formations on either flank, who could detach men to
bolster the front flank if theirs was not under attack.
Beyond this, while the breastwork obstructions
facing the ravine may not have been as formidable
as those on the flanks and rear, the steep slope of
the ravine had a natural sub-surface of ice and com-
pacted snow, which according to some accounts

A modern (2013) view of the site of the Battle of the
Longwoods from the vantage point of the American
defences. The modern paved and straightened road
passes to the upper left, while the remnant of the
old road can be traced curving down into the ravine
towards the old bridge location at the centre.

The small but strategically important creek at the
bottom of the ravine.

The view of the American position from the bottom of the ravine. The embankment to the right is the result of later infilling of the ravine to create the current road, however, the steep banks directly ahead trace the original slope.

had been enhanced by the Americans by pouring water down the slope to freeze in the frigid air. As a result, the column's impetus on the downward trek was rapidly eliminated and disrupted as it tried to force its way up the ice-bound rise, with men unable to gain any traction in their leather-soled boots. Furthermore, as a solid mass of men it represented a perfect unmissable target for the American soldiers, only a matter of yards away and producing the heaviest volume of firing that could be brought to bear. According to the American commander, Holmes:

> The enemy threw his militia and Natives across the ravine above the road and commenced an action with bugles…. His regulars at the same time charged down the road from the opposite heights, crossed the bridge, charged up the heights we occupied, within twenty steps of the American line and against the most destructive fire. But his front section was shot to pieces. Those who followed were much thinned and wounded. His officers were soon cut down…. He therefore abandoned the charge and took cover in the woods at diffused order, between fifteen and twenty paces of our line, and placed all hope upon his ammunition.[10]

This view gives clear indication of the obstacle the British troops had to overcome in their attempts to come to grips with their foes and the dominant advantage the Americans held on the high ground.

While Basden recorded:

The enemy commenced their fire immediately upon our appearance, and when the head of the column had proceeded a short distance down the hill, the firing from them [the Americans] was so severe as to occasion a check. They [the column] however, instantly cheered and rushed on, making for the road on the opposite side, with the intention of carrying this fence. However, this was found impossible, the ascent being so steep and slippery.[11]

Taking increasing numbers of casualties in this close-packed formation, Basden attempted to deploy his sections into a line, with the 1st (Royal Scots) on the left and 89th on the right. By this he hoped to reduce his casualties and extend the width of his attack. Unfortunately, the rough and slippery ground bordering the creek disrupted any coherent linear formation and each time an advance was attempted by the separate sections, the slippery incline destroyed any cohesion as men slid back or fell, while those who succeeded in advancing simply became more prominent targets for the American guns and were shot down.

Unable to break through as a body, most of the attackers fell back across the creek and began firing from the cover of fallen trees scattered across the slope of the ravine, others, however, remained just below the American position, resulting in the aforementioned stalemate of firing at ranges of sometimes less than twenty yards (18 meters).

Looking to break the impasse, Basden collected whatever men he could locate and directed them to "follow me and I moved in the ravine to the right for some distance under an uncommon severe fire."[12] Reaching a point he thought well beyond the left end of the American line, Basden believed his force of regulars and Natives could climb the embankment and, after forming on the open ground above, attack the enemy on a vulnerable open flank. Instead, "on ascending and gaining the top of the bank, I was very much surprised to observe another face of a work."[13] Immediately upon the appearance of this new target, the American troops lining the American left flank (north face), namely the Twenty-Sixth Vermont Militia and Twenty-Seventh New York State Militia, opened fire. In response, Basden stated:

> I placed the men in extended order under cover of the trees, and the action was kept up with great vigour till dusk.... I now determined to send to the point on the top of the hill ... for more men to strengthen the party I had then with me, and upon their arrival, to storm the enemy's position agreeably to my first intention.[14]

However, no such attack took place as "At this instant I received a severe wound in my thigh, and was under the necessity of going to the rear."[15]

Command of the disorganized British force now devolved upon Ensign Francis Miles (89th Regiment) who, not having any idea how the militia forces on the other side of the American position were faring (in fact, they too had come under heavy American fire and been reduced to sniping from the surrounding wood line), but knowing his own force was effectively blockaded, made no additional attempts to close with the enemy in the deepening darkness. Instead, the various British and Canadian detachments broke off and retired to the east side of the ravine, just in time to meet up with Lieutenant Colonel Stewart and a detachment of reserve troops, who had just hurried up the last few miles of their exhausting march in response to the sounds of battle echoing across the frozen countryside. Unable to see or assess the American positions or numbers in the darkness, and with his own force clearly severely traumatized and reduced, Stewart ordered a retreat to the Fourteen Mile Creek, there to remain on the alert throughout the night before assessing the tactical situation in the light of day.

Looking to mitigate the serious defeat his troops had suffered whilst he was absent from command, Stewart immediately penned his version of the day's events (including the reversal of the flanks upon which the militias and Natives served) and an initial casualty list,[16] before dispatching it to Major General Riall at Burlington Heights.

However, following this, he failed to maintain any effective rearguard watch on the Americans. As a result, despite receiving word that the enemy were apparently retreating, he made no effort to

ESTIMATE OF CASUALTIES, BATTLE OF THE LONGWOODS, MARCH 4, 1814[16]

British

Regulars
Killed: 2 officer, 12 rank and file
Wounded: 2 officers, 1 sergeant, 38 rank and file
Missing/
Prisoner: 1 bugler, 1 volunteer

Loyal Kent Volunteers
Wounded: 1 officer, 1 sergeant, 5 rank and file

American[18]

Killed: 4 all ranks
Wounded: 4 all ranks

re-establish contact until the following morning, when his scouts found Holmes' camp abandoned:

> Sir — I have to acquaint you that the enemy retreated precipiantly from their position about 8 o'clock on the night of the 4th instant down the River Thames. As the service for which the advance of the troops was intended has been frustrated by the Natives refusing to proceed with the ammunition, and no probability of our being able to come up with the enemy,

as they had gained twelve hours' march of us, I have withdrawn the troops to this place [Delaware] where we will remain waiting your further instructions.[17]
—Stewart to Riall, March 6, 1814

In fact, following the engagement, and after spirited discussion amongst the various American officers as to their tactical position and fighting capability due to casualties, they agreed to make an immediate silent retreat under the cover of the night, allowing them to be well back on their march to Detroit before Stewart reacted to their departure. Upon his return to Detroit and submitting his casualty report,[*18] Holmes came under some criticism for retreating, to which he made the following rebuttal in a report to Lieutenant Colonel Butler.

I did not pursue for the following reasons:

1. We had triumphed against numbers and discipline and were therefore under no obligation of honor to incur additional hazard.

2. ... the enemy were still superior [in numbers] and the night would have insured success to ambuscade.

3. The enemy's bugle sounded close upon the opposite heights. If then we pursued, we must have passed over to him as he did to us, because the creek could be passed on horseback at no other point, and the troops, being fatigued and frost bitten, their shoes cut to pieces by frozen ground, it was not possible to pursue on foot.[19]

In the aftermath of this small but decisive engagement, the Americans pushed forward yet another force of around 500 men up the Thames Valley around the middle of March, advancing as far as the upper reaches of the Thames and once more raiding farmsteads. They also sought to recover the guns and wagons previously hidden by Holmes' column, but without success. This failure was simply because in the intervening period three men from the Loyal Essex Volunteers militia, who had escaped from being held at Amherstburg and were returning to Port Talbot, had found the hidden stash. Taking what supplies were useful, the militiamen reached safety and then returned with a party of their fellow militiamen; whereupon they disabled the wagons by removing their wheels, burned the artillery carriages, and hauled off the cannon barrels and ammunition, hiding them deep in the nearby Black Ash Swamp, where they supposedly remained to the end of the war. Nonetheless, news of this latest American incursion

The small monument dedicated to the Battle of the Longwoods, located alongside the modern rural road Highway 2.

alarmed Major General Riall, who decided to abandon his advanced positions in the London district and concentrate his forces at Oxford, with other detachments stationed at Port Talbot, Long Point, Turkey Point, Dover, and Burford. As a result, the intervening region was left fully exposed to future American incursions. Fortunately the intermittent thaws with the onset of spring degenerated the roads to an even worse state of repair than normal, forcing both sides to suspend their offensive activities until the weather and road conditions improved enough for campaigning to recommence.

CHAPTER 4

Marching in a New Direction — Or Two

To many Americans, the combination of the devastation inflicted on Buffalo at the end of December 1813 and the continued British occupation of Fort Niagara created a nationalistic call for retribution and recapture. However, for the military planners the relative importance of eliminating Kingston initially relegated the Niagara frontier to a secondary objective. To this end, in coordination with the resurgence of Sackets Harbor as the focus of American military activity on the Northern frontier, Secretary of War John Armstrong issued an order for Major General Brown to leave his winter encampment at French Mills and make a forced march to Sackets Harbor with some 2,000 men. He also provided Brown with information that the British were supposedly planning to move a significant number of troops out of Kingston, leaving that place vulnerable to attack:

> … a moment may occur in which you may do, with the aid of Commodore Chauncey, what I last year intended Pike should have done … viz: to cross the river, or head of the lake on the ice, and carry Kingston by a coup de main. This is not, however, to be attempted, but under a combination of the following circumstances: practicable roads, good weather, large detachments (made westerly) on the part of the enemy, and a full and hearty co-operation on the part of our own naval commander.[1]
>
> — Armstrong to Brown,
> February 28, 1814

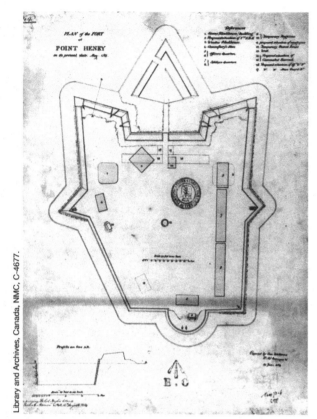

Plan of the Fort at Point Henry. Originally drafted in May 1813, this map copy was made up in June 1814 and includes additional structures and fortifications proposed to be added as part of the overall strengthening of Kingston's defences. In the post-war era, this fortification was entirely replaced by the massive citadel that exists today. The only surviving feature of the original fort is the well (number 13 on the map and located at the centre of the main parade square).

Fort Henry, J. E. Woolford, artist, 1821. The strategically dominant position of Fort Henry is clearly seen in this post-war view across the St. Lawrence River.

Armstrong also provided Brown with a set of false orders, apparently ordering Brown to march to the Niagara frontier, link up with Brigadier General Winfield Scott, and attack Fort Niagara. This decoy document was to be deliberately leaked to the British, thus distracting their attentions toward the Niagara, while the real American attack occurred at Kingston.

> If the enterprise be agreed upon, use the enclosed letter [No. 2] to mask your object and let no one into your secret but Chauncey …
> [No. 2]
> (Intended to deceive the enemy)

Kingston, 1815, E.E. Vidal, artist, 1815. This image is a detail taken from a larger painting and shows Fort Henry as the Americans would have seen it from their ships.

Sir — Colonel Scott, who is in nomination as a brigadier has orders to repair to the Niagara frontier and to take with him a corps of artillerists and a battering and field train &c. Major Wood, of the engineers, and Dallaba, of the ordnance, will accompany, or follow him. Four hundred Natives, and about four thousand volunteer militia are under similar orders. The truth is that public opinion will no longer tolerate us in permitting the enemy to keep quiet possession of Fort Niagara. Another motive is the effect which may be expected from the appearance of a large corps on the Niagara, in restraining the enemy's enterprises westward of that point.[2]

— Armstrong to Brown,
February 28, 1814

Unfortunately, Armstrong's scheme came to nothing, as:

- intervals of abnormally warm weather and high winds during late February 1814 caused the ice on Lake Ontario to break up earlier than normal;

- Chauncey proved reluctant to co-operate with Brown, as he believed it would force him to submit to the demands of the army instead of maintaining an independent naval force; and
- the British stubbornly refused to co-operate by moving their troops out of Kingston.

Claiming that the conditions for an attack on Kingston had not been met, Commodore Chauncey persuaded Major General Brown that instead of being a ruse, the second letter from Armstrong was, in fact, an alternative set of orders. Following this supposed alternate command, Brown's army began

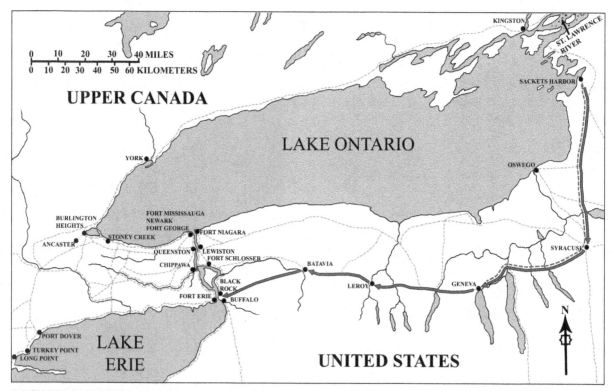

BROWN'S EXTENDED MARCH TO NIAGARA

The repetitive route taken by General Brown's forces in order to reach the Niagara frontier in March 1814.

its advance toward the Niagara in early March. Upon reaching the town of Geneva, some 130 miles (209 kilometers) from Sackets Harbor, Brown was met by Brigadier General Edmund Gaines, who corrected Brown's erroneous implementation of the second letter and recommended Brown return to Sackets Harbor. Somewhat confused, Brown drafted a letter to Armstrong asking for clarification of his orders and marched his troops back to Sackets Harbor, only to be immediately assailed by Chauncey, who pressured him once more to believe that his march on the Niagara frontier was the correct interpretation of the document. Brown therefore proceeded to take his exhausted troops back over the same route they had already marched twice before, toward Geneva. Finally, on April 8, 1814, Armstrong's reply caught up with Major General Brown, clarifying that the second letter was a deliberate phoney, intended only to deceive the British, but since Brown had already acted on it, "If you hazard anything by this mistake, correct it promptly by returning to your post. If on the other hand you left the Harbor with a competent force for its defence, go on and prosper. Good consequences are sometimes the result of mistakes...."[3]

As a result, Major General Brown and his footsore army finally reached the Niagara frontier on April 14, 1814, just in time to experience a late winter storm that dumped almost nine inches (24 centimeters) of wet snow on the proposed site of the encampment, overlooking the Niagara River and near the ruins of Buffalo. Within days of this arrival, however, Brown received reports that the British had launched their new, larger warships at Kingston and that the associated build-up of troops and supplies were intended for use in a renewed pre-emptive attack on Chauncey's fleet before it could emerge onto the lake. In response, Major General Brown decided to return to Sackets Harbour, the site of his previous (self-proclaimed) victory, to oversee its defence and possibly add to his own glory. Instead, once there, Brown found himself effectively trapped and forced to wait with increasing impatience for an attack that did not materialize — as every intelligence and spying report he received said it should.

CHAPTER 5

The Attack That Never Was

Considering the amount of intelligence the British had accumulated about activities at Sackets Harbor, the fact that they failed to make a pre-emptive strike to destroy the new American fleet while it was still unfinished and the military advantage of the moment was decidedly in their favour has been criticized by some historians as a critical lapse that significantly affected the development and end-result of the campaigns to come. Admittedly, there is some validity in this argument; but the blame can certainly not be laid at the feet of the local commanders, Lieutenant General Gordon Drummond and Sir James Yeo, as for once their assessment of the strategic situation and the necessity of making just such an attack were synchronized. Instead, and once again, the proverbial "fly in the ointment" was Sir George Prevost's determination to maintain his priority of defending Lower Canada.

By March 1814, Yeo's two new frigates, the *Princess Charlotte* and *Prince Regent*, were almost ready to be launched and all of the requisite additional fittings were stockpiled on the dockside. Similarly, the new gunboats, *Nelly*, *Lais*, and *Cleopatra*, were already fully fitted-out and ready for action, while the "old" fleet, under new names, had all been refitted as ordered. In addition, the arrival of significant detachments of experienced seamen, drawn or transferred from warships and Royal Navy transports on the east coast, would serve to crew the fleet when it sailed. In the meantime the men were effectively restricted to their quarters at Point Frederick and Point Henry, to the frustration of the local shopkeepers. On the other hand, the ship's officers were more freely able to visit Kingston to provide custom to the merchants and opportunity to the town's matrons with eligible daughters.

Conversely, the reports emerging from Sackets Harbor were becoming more and more alarming to Yeo, as they revealed the accelerating and expanding scale of the American efforts to complete the building of their two new brigs (subsequently named the *Jefferson* and *Jones*). This was backed by the prospect of one or two new behemoth frigates (subsequently named *Superior* and *Mohawk*), following right behind in the production schedule. In addition, there were details of additional land defences being constructed and extra troops being put on the march to swell the garrison, then under Brigadier General Edmund Gaines. Time was running out before the sailing season began, and the longer nothing was done the more likely it became that the Americans would not only catch up but surpass the initial British lead. Especially when intelligence revealed that, in addition to what had already arrived, there was a constant flow of convoys and wagon trains of shipbuilding supplies and armaments (especially long-barrelled cannon) passing along an overland and river-based supply route that ultimately led to the warehouse staging post at Oswego, on the south side of Lake Ontario. From there, these shipments were being ferried up by boats that hugged the American shore to Sackets Harbor. Yeo was therefore in no doubt that a pre-emptive strike, first on Sackets Harbor and then Oswego, was an essential operational priority. However, Drummond saw things differently and believed the priority was to send shipments of arms, equipment, ammunition, food, and reinforcements up to York, Burlington, and the Niagara frontier aboard Yeo's ships, as soon as possible, before any operation took place against the American bases.

The two commanders eventually met and worked out a mutually beneficial compromise. Their first target would be to attack and destroy Sackets Harbor, using a landing force of over 4,000 troops, backed by Yeo's entire fleet as fire support. They would follow-up with a similar amphibious assault on Oswego, thus eliminating the two main American bases on eastern Lake Ontario, destroying Chauncey's fleet before it became too formidable a threat, and cutting the principal supply line leading to the increasing number of American troops now being reported as mustering at the camps outside of Buffalo on the Niagara. Once this was achieved, Yeo would then reciprocate by using his fleet as a fast transports for the new and full-strength regiments, weapons, ammunition, and supplies Drummond wanted to push forward and to return with the exhausted and depleted remnants of the regiments that had thus far shouldered the burden of fighting for the previous twenty-two months on the Niagara frontier. Drummond also showed Yeo a communication he had previously received from Prevost outlining events involving the respective governments of the two warring countries and its likely impact on their plans.

According to the letter, following the January agreement between Britain and the United States to formally undertake peace negotiations, the Americans had forwarded a subsequent notice to Prevost's attention (through the person of Brigadier General Winder), proposing a mutual cessation of hostilities and the holding of meetings to conclude an armistice that would continue until the results of the negotiations were known. Having constantly been under pressure from his own superiors to remain on the defensive in the pressing of the war in North America and not to provide the Americans with any unifying issue that could escalate hostilities, Prevost took this offer very seriously and passed it on to his subordinates for their assessment — with the added implication that he anticipated their concurrence that negotiations should begin as soon as possible and that no offensive action that could jeopardize these talks should take place.

Lieutenant General Drummond had already replied, stating:

I beg leave most respectfully to submit as my opinion, that the object of Mr Monroe's letter is twofold. First, To gain time for organizing their Naval and Military Force. Second, To cause the proposal for the Armistice, (the discussion of which is to afford that time,) to originate with Your Excellency. — Unless Your Excellency is in possession of some other pledge than Brigadier General Winder's assurity of the sincerity of his Government, I should place but little faith in them; as [he] ... is one of the most strenuous supporters of the War ... We should be extremely cautious in doing anything [to give] the Enemy the smallest reason to infer ... [our willingness] ... to court, or even too willingly to meet, his advances for a cessation of hostilities. — [because] ... the whole of the advantages ... to be derived from the Armistice will be reaped by the enemy ... Should an opportunity offer, by even a temporary naval superiority, for the destruction of the Enemy's Fleet, and Arsenal, at Sackett's Harbour, a vigorous combined attack by the Navy and Army would be highly advisable ... [followed by] ...

the pushing of troops ... Stores, etc, to the relief of Fort Niagara and the Right Division.[1]

— Drummond to Prevost,
April 2, 1814

After reading the letter, Yeo sent off his own assessment without hesitation:

After the most deliberate consideration, I am of the opinion that, as far as it relates to Naval operations ... to be decidedly of the opinion that were Your Excellency to accept of the proposed Armistice — it would neither conduce to the credit of His Majesty's Government or the Honor of his Arms; — While it would enable the Enemy to gain time for the launching & equipping more ships — augmenting & concentrating his forces & bring them to bear (should a rupture of the Armistice ensue — a measure, I fear, from the known enmity & insincerity of the American Government, too likely to occur) with redoubled force against us.[2]

— Yeo to Prevost, April 13, 1814

Coincidentally, Yeo's response was sent on the same day Drummond forwarded the agreed combined operations plan for the attack on Sackets Harbor to Prevost. However, such was the confidence of the two commanders — they were sure that despite their having just contradicted their superior by their strong opposition to an armistice, the obvious necessity of the attack and the sense of their proposal would bring an immediate approval in reply. This confidence went so far that they had proceeded with their assembly of the necessary transport craft, landing boats, supplies, armaments, and ammunition, while drafting movement orders for the appropriate crews and regiments already in Upper Canada that were to be involved in the attack. The only external factor being that the plan needed some 4,000 men to ensure success. This number was far more than were at or near Kingston, or even beyond the total that could be raised by taking the dangerous chance of removing troops and support artillery from Prescott, York, and the Niagara frontier, thus temporarily weakening both those flanks. The only answer, therefore, was that Prevost was going to have to ante up around 800 to 1,000 troops from Lower Canada to get the essential job done.

As they had hoped, the answer came back quickly, but it was not what they expected. Instead of simply agreeing or even rejecting their proposal, Sir George first ridiculed their estimates and plans and then proposed his own outline for an attack on the American base. First, Yeo and his fleet would sail and establish a blockade of Sackets Harbor to trap the American vessels in port. They would then undertake a shore bombardment to support Drummond when his (far smaller than originally proposed and composed entirely of Upper Canada-sourced troops) infantry and artillery force made their overland attack from the north after crossing the St. Lawrence River and making a rapid forced march south to take the Americans from behind. This extraordinary counter-proposal shocked both commanders, as it would not only require an entirely different series of logistics and a difficult degree of coordination (as the two elements came from completely different directions and without any effective real-time coordinating communications), but it would also be a sufficiently smaller size that victory could not be ensured. Why Prevost advanced this proposal is not conclusively known, but as Drummond's current plan closely mirrored the one implemented but not successfully followed through upon by Prevost the previous May (for details see *The Pendulum of War*), there are grounds to suspect that any victory with this similar plan and under Drummond would have become an implicit further criticism of Prevost's lack of success when he was in command.

In reply, Drummond made a bold and forthright reiteration of his previous arguments.

Sir, I have the honor to acknowledge the receipt of Your Excellencys Letter … enclosing a plan of a combined attack to be made on the Enemy's fleet at Sackett's Harbour, to which I have given that serious attention which the great importance the subject demands.

By my letter sent to Your Excellency of yesterday's date, written prior to the arrival of your dispatches … you will perceive that I had already in a great measure anticipated Your Excellency's views with regard to the imperious necessity which exists for an *immediate* attempt to destroy the Enemy's fleet, at the same time, I now beg leave to repeat, that in my opinion a force of not less than 4,000 effective troops would be necessary to ensure a reasonable hope of success…. I had a communication with Sir James Yeo relative to the expediency of [your plan for] … a combined attack on the Enemys fleet. I also … had a meeting with him this morning on the same subject, when I submitted to him Your Excellency's letter and its accompanying document. Sir James entirely coincides in opinion with me that the force to be brought against the place ought to at least what I have before stated.... In addition to the operation in agitation against Sackett's Harbour, I conceive that a successful attack on their great Naval depot at Oswego would nearly, if not altogether, circumscribe the proceedings of the enemy.... I propose giving Sir James Yeo an adequate number of Troops, to cooperate with him for the accomplishment of this desirable object, as soon after the Squadron can put to sea, as possible.[3]

— Drummond to Prevost,
Noon, April 27, 1814

Prevost obviously did not miss the implied criticism or tones of Drummond's letters, nor the rejections made by both commanders over the earlier proposed armistice, as he made clear in his quickly returned reply, dated April 30, 1814.

In your despatch[es] ... I perceive a more decided opinion on the contemplated movement against Sackett's Harbour — You consider that a land force to be employed on this service should not be less than four thousand effective Rank and File, to afford a reasonable hope of success.... But the fact is, that the force in this country is insufficient to enable me to concentrate at any one point in Upper Canada, the numbers of regulars you require for this important service, without stripping Lower Canada of nearly the whole of those that are present within it, and committing its defence to Provincials and Militia — The views of His Majesty's Government respecting the mode of conducting the war with America do not justify my exposing too much on one stake — It is by wary measures and occasional daring enterprizes with apparently disproportionate means, that the character of the War has been sustained, and from that policy I am not disposed to depart. From a presumption that the Government of the United States is animated by a sincere desire of an armistice ... I have been induced to accede to the President's proposal of appointing an Officer of Rank to discuss and arrange tomorrow ... the Articles of a suspension of Arms — This circumstances renders it inexpedient that an offensive movement against any of the Enemy's positions should be undertaken until you shall again hear from me on the subject ... .You will please to communicate to Commodore Sir James Yeo, the subject of this letter, but I do not wish it to restrain him from any operations he may have in view until the Armistice shall be officially announced.[4]

— Prevost to Drummond,
April 30, 1814

Drummond received this blunt veto of the Sackets Harbor operation on May 3rd, and immediately conferred with Yeo. Because Drummond was Prevost's subordinate officer and Prevost would not send up any troops to support the Sackets Harbor plan, there was nothing Drummond could hope to do that would have a reasonable hope of success against that prime target. In addition, his notification that he was going ahead with armistice negotiations, in direct opposition to the adamant recommendations of both officers, was an open slap in the face to their authorities, experience, and dignities. However, reading between the lines, Prevost had also implicitly recognized that while he could order Drummond not to do anything, his authority no longer applied to Yeo.

It should therefore come as no surprise that within twenty-four hours the British squadron had sailed from Kingston to the sounds of cheering crowds and exchanged cannon salutes from the ships and shore batteries, and with the vessel's

---

BRITISH FORCES ASSIGNED TO THE RAID ON OSWEGO, MAY 5–6, 1814[5]

British Fleet

Princess Charlotte (Captain William Mulcaster)
Prince Regent (Captain Richard O'Conor)
Montreal (ex *Wolfe*) (Captain Stephen Popham)
Magnet (ex *Sir Sidney Smith*) (Commander E. Collier)
Niagara (ex *Royal George*) (Captain Francis Spilsbury)
Charwell (ex *Earl of Moria*) (Captain Alexander Dobbs)
Star (ex *Lord Melville*) (Captain C. Anthony or Commander Charles Owen)
Plus an unspecified number of gunboats and bateaux
Landing Force (Lieutenant Colonel Fischer)
De Watteville Regiment (Lieutenant Colonel Fischer) est. 450 rank and file
Glengarry Light Infantry Regiment (Captain McMillan) est. 50 rank and file
Royal Marines, 2nd Battalion (Lieutenant Colonel Malcolm) est. 400 rank and file
Royal Artillery (1 x 12-lbr, brass, 1 x 5 ½ inch Howitzer) (Captain Cruttenden) est. 24 gunners
Royal Marine Artillery, Rocket Company (Lieutenant Stevens) est. 6 rocketeers
Royal Sappers and Miners (detachment) (Lieutenant Gosset, Royal Engineers) est. 20 rank and file
Royal Navy, volunteer seamen, est. 200 all ranks
Estimated combined total 1,200 All Ranks

decks filled with Drummond's troops!"[5] Behind him, Drummond left behind his latest regular report for dispatch to Prevost, which again reiterated his strong conviction that a full-scale operation against Sackets Harbor was essential to safeguard Upper Canada and he that hoped Prevost would change his mind — but in the meantime, and until he heard back, he and Yeo would continue with their time-sensitive and preplanned operation against Oswego.

CHAPTER 6

The Raid on Oswego, May 5–6, 1814

The target of the British sortie was the old British defensive depot officially designated as Fort Ontario, but known generally as Fort Oswego. Built in 1759 to replace an earlier structure destroyed during the Seven Years War between Britain and France, Fort Oswego commanded the strategic entrance to the Oswego River and a line of communications leading south to the Mohawk Valley. It was through this corridor that the great majority of the supplies destined for Sackets Harbor were being channelled and its elimination would, in the British commanders' views, be of significant value in throttling the development of Chauncey's warships at Sackets Harbor.

Prior to the current war, the depot and fort had been an isolated and insignificant outpost, and was allowed to deteriorate to a state of dereliction. Once the war began the warehouses had been repaired, but the fort remained an effective ruin and the garrison of troops little more than a watch guard. Now, in 1814, with the huge building program taking place at Sackets Harbor, Oswego took on new significance as a focal point for the transfer of supplies. Consequently, by the end of April the existing garrison of twenty-five seamen (Lieutenant George Pearce) had been supplemented by a force of around 300 artillerists from the Third Artillery Regiment (Lieutenant Colonel George Mitchell). Unfortunately, despite their strong numbers, they brought no field pieces with them, as they were expected to use the ones listed as being on-site. However, upon arrival these were found to be only five derelict pieces, without carriages and with three having had their trunnions (elevating swivels) sawn off (to designate them as condemned). Furthermore, the supposed defensive fortifications on the hilltop were effectively useless, with the wooden picket walls mainly rotted away and collapsed into the ditch.

While repairing the five guns and beginning temporary repairs to the picketing, the American garrison was alarmed when, shortly after dawn on May 5th, a flotilla of ships and gunboats, all towing longboats and bateaux, were seen approaching from the north. Knowing the American fleet was still in harbour, the titular garrison commander, Commandant Melancthon Woolsey, quickly identified them as British and sent riders into the surrounding communities to muster and bring back as many militia that could be assembled before the inevitable attack descended. He also issued orders that the small schooners *Growler* and *Penelope*, moored at the wharf below the fort, be prepared to be scuttled if necessary. Curiously, although there was a surplus of artillerymen available and no less than twelve large cannon and a wealth of shot and powder immediately on hand that could be jury-rigged for action, even if it was only for a single round, these guns were not brought into service. Thus, apart from erecting a number of tents on the flat ground below the fort to give the impression that there was an enhanced number in the defenders force, nothing was done to enhance the defences of the position. Instead,

these valuable guns and shot were ordered dumped into the Oswego River, while the surplus artillerymen were designated for duty as infantrymen.

Aboard the arriving flotilla, preparations were being made to land by noon. The plan was for Lieutenant Colonel Fischer to lead the initial landing force — composed of two companies of his De Watteville Regiment, some Royal Marines, and the detachment of the Glengarry Light Infantry — to a position on the left (east) of the fort and attack uphill from there. At the same time, Lieutenant Colonel Malcolm would lead the remaining bulk of the 2nd Battalion of Royal Marines, backed by 200 volunteer sailors under Captain Mulcaster, in a landing to the right (west) of the fort, thus splitting the enemy's firepower. The remaining four companies of De Wattevilles and artillery were to remain onboard the fleet and act as a mobile reserve or secondary landing column if required.

To commence the operation, a number of the shallow-draft gunboats were sent inshore with orders to bombard the enemy positions and draw retaliatory fire, so as to reveal the American positions. One of the derelict American guns mounted at the fort burst its barrel when fired, leaving the fort with only four guns (a 4-pounder and 9-pounder facing the lake and two 4-pounders facing the inland flank). Following this initial foray, the landing craft began loading late in the afternoon, with a projected landing to take place before sunset. However, within the space of a couple of hours the weather had changed dramatically as a storm front blew in, whipping up a wind that threatened to drive the entire fleet onto the nearby shore and creating decidedly choppy conditions in which the already overloaded small boats and bateaux were in serious danger of being swamped. Left with little alternative if he was to safeguard his entire brand-new fleet, Yeo was forced to call off the landing, order the troops re-embarked, and then see the fleet weigh anchor and reposition itself further offshore, where they could manoeuvre without the danger of being wrecked. So rapidly was this done and so imminent was the danger perceived to be, that once the troops were re-boarded at least four of the bateaux and boats were cast adrift instead of being secured (and thereby possibly becoming a floating anchor to their respective boats if they became swamped in the expected storm).

Despite being given this unexpected and heaven-sent reprieve, the Americans made little additional effort to improve their defensive positions or remove any of the vital supplies. Fortunately, as the night passed, detachments of around 200 local militia arrived to supplement the garrison's numbers and were posted alongside the detachments of artillery men acting as infantry on the low wooded ground to the east of the fort, near the tent encampment, as it was anticipated that this was where the enemy would land.

Later that night the threat of the storm had passed, but due to headwinds the fleet took some time to tack up to its proper stations. Once there, the landing boats were secured alongside and the first contingents of men clambered down the ships sides in the pre-dawn darkness. At dawn the attack recommenced, with the fleet beginning an intensive bombardment of the identified American positions that did no real damage nor inflicted significant casualties. However, it did succeed in persuading many of the just-arrived militia that this was no place to remain, causing almost the entire contingent to desert forthwith. Meanwhile, offshore the continuing choppy conditions and brisk wind slowed the completion of the loading of the boats until well after noon, forcing many of the men who had boarded first to be tossed about for hours on end. Finally, shortly before 2:00 p.m., the two flotillas of boats pulled for the shore, with Fischer's contingent aiming for the American tented encampment and apparently flat shoreline to the east of the fort. What was not taken into account, however, was that this position had an extensive and uneven shoal of rocks just offshore, below the surface of the water. This impediment grounded many of the heavily laden boats and bateaux well

The Storming of Fort Oswego by 2nd Battalion Royal Marines and a party of Seamen, 15m past Twelve at noon, R. Havell & Son engravers, published in 1817. This engraving was produced from an original sketch done by Captain William Steele.

away from the beach, forcing their troops to jump into the water and flounder ashore while under fire. In addition, due to the broken nature of the lakebed, the shallows were intermingled with deeper stretches of water that dunked many a man who unwarily stepped into them — soaking and ruining their cartridge boxes of ammunition. Reaching the shore, the landed troops began to form their company lines and assess the damage done to their supply of ammunition (while still under fire). After distributing the available usable ammunition it was discovered that each man would only have a handful of shots to attack with. For Fischer this posed a dilemma, as their reserve ammunition was to have been brought in the succeeding wave of boats and would take some time to arrive, while the other landing force was already approaching its landing zone off to the right and directly below the fort. If he delayed his own advance to obtain a resupply of ammunition, Fischer knew that Malcolm's Marines and Mulcaster's naval volunteers would take the full brunt of the American fire from the fort. He therefore made the difficult decision to give as many of the usable cartridges as could be spared to the detachment of around fifty Glengarry Light Infantry that was with his landing force. They were then ordered to move off to the left and enter the woods from which the Americans were firing and, without knowing the strength of the enemy before them (somewhere between one and two hundred men), to clear that ground of any opposition. At the same time, the remaining troops from the De Watteville Regiment would advance toward the fort, armed solely with the bayonets that were now fixed on the ends of their otherwise-useless muskets.

Meanwhile, on the right of the British landing, the Marines and naval volunteers landed against minimal resistance and advanced up the steeper slope of the hillside, only to come up against an increasing level of American fire as men retreating from the eastern flank reached the relative security of the fort and bolstered the defensive position. Despite this, the poor state of the fort's structural defences and woefully under-gunned garrison left the issue in little doubt and, despite putting up a strong defence, once the British Marines and sailors succeeded in breaching the fort's earthwork perimeter, Mitchell was forced to order the evacuation and retreat of his remaining forces into the nearby woods.

The British had won the day, but at a relatively heavy cost.[1] They then began the principal reason for their attack by stripping the adjacent warehouses of whatever supplies could be transported and destroying the remainder. They also refloated the scuttled boats and towed them out as prizes of war. However, the volume of materiel found at the port did not match what was expected if the intelligence reports were correct. Believing that the Americans may have removed and hidden the missing items during the British fleet's unexpected withdrawal, Drummond had a search made of the surrounding forest, while Yeo questioned some of the prisoners to gain the required information, but in both cases to no avail. In fact, the greater bulk of the supplies were still in transit and were only a few miles upriver, stored at the American depots at Fredericksburg and Three River Point.

Left and above: Details from the engraving, showing the vessels involved as part of the British fleet and the final storming of the fort.

However, without knowing of these supplies, Yeo and Drummond, while recognizing that they had at least put a dent in Chauncey's program of construction, were aware that the victory could rightly be criticized for suffering such heavy casualties against a relatively weak garrison position and the far fewer-than-expected supplies gained. It would also bring into question the certainty of a victory in any future attack against Sackets Harbor, where the defences were substantially stronger and the garrison vastly greater. As a result, once they had returned to Kingston to a hero's welcome on May 8th, both commanders submitted reports that enhanced the state and strengths of the American defences, exaggerated their defender's numbers, and over-estimated the significance of the impact it would have upon the American building efforts at Sackets Harbor. However, they need not have worried about criticism from Prevost, as he was occupied with the deteriorating prospects of concluding an armistice with the Americans at Plattsburg.

There, Prevost's representative, Colonel Baynes, had been fully expecting to meet with Brigadier

ESTIMATE OF CASUALTIES, RAID ON OSWEGO, MAY 5–6, 1814[1]

British Troops
Killed: 1 officer, 2 sergeants, 1 drummer, 11 rank and file
Wounded: 2 officers, 2 sergeants, 9 rank and file

Naval Ratings
Killed: 2 seamen
Wounded: 2 officers, 3 seamen

Royal Marines
Killed: 1 officer, 2 sergeants, 3 rank and file
Wounded: 1 officer, 1 sergeant, 22 rank and file

American
Killed: 1 officer, 20 rank and file
Prisoners: 25 rank and file

(N.B., the American account for this engagement listed 6 killed, 38 wounded, and 25 prisoners, all ranks.)

However, the designated American representative, Brigadier General Winder, did not turn up. Instead, the subordinate American representative, Colonel Ninian Pinkney, arrived with the contradictory claims that while he was empowered to discuss the imposition of restrictions upon British warships operating off the eastern seaboard (something over which Prevost had no jurisdiction), he had no authority to negotiate anything on land other than a local ceasefire and termination on a twenty-day notice. In fact, he considered himself so restricted in his jurisdiction in that sphere that he refused to open the official dispatch pouch from Washington (containing instructions for the negotiations), because it was addressed to Brigadier General Winder!

Unable to make any headway and believing that he was simply being stalled, Baynes returned to report the breakdown of negotiations to Prevost. In the aftermath of having Drummond and Yeo's warnings seemingly proved true, it is possible to conclude that by writing the following letter, Prevost may have looked to recover some of his authority in the face of their unauthorized venture (while at the same time covering himself in case of subsequent criticism for not supporting their proposed attack on Sackets Harbor), by retroactively claiming to have approved the expedition to Oswego and then establishing a documented

General Winder. He had also come with a full brief of terms and proposals that would have seen the armistice applied across the entire theatre of war on the Northern frontier, be indefinite in length, and subject to expiry only after a fifty-day notice of the failure of the negotiations in Europe or an equivalent notice from their respective governments.

new tone and position on the question of sending troops into Upper Canada.

> My letter to you of the same date [May 3rd] will have anticipated your wishes by conveying my approval of that measure. I cannot at this moment supply you with the 800 effective men you deem necessary to enable you to attempt, by a combined operation, the destruction of the enemy's fleet and stores at Sackets Harbor, and it will depend upon the force which His Majesty's Government may place at my disposal from England during the next month, whether the seat of war may be transferred to the enemy's possessions contiguous to Upper Canada, or whether, as at present is the case, I shall be obliged to retain the whole of the troops I have in Lower Canada for its defence.[2]
>
> —Prevost to Drummond,
> May 7, 1813

At the same time, on the American side of the lake the loss of Oswego and, more importantly, the loss of some of the important, guns, fittings, and supplies destined for the new vessels at Sackets Harbor, caused Commodore Chauncey to react with exaggerated measures for the protection of his additional deliveries. In the short-term, a strong body of troops were transferred from Sackets Harbor to Oswego with instructions to fortify the position and then salvage as much as possible from what had been left behind or missed by the British, and see it taken upriver to Fredericksburg where it would join the supplies at that depot — which, despite the logistical and transport difficulties and inevitable damages and loss of time involved, were now to be transported overland to Sackets Harbor. He also ordered the acceleration of his already strained program of building. The *Superior* had been launched on May 1st, and was being fitted-out with every piece of equipment that could be found, scrounged, or expropriated from the warehouses and other vessels in the harbour, while the frames and planking for the new vessel *Mohawk* were being constructed in a round-the-clock schedule. There are also indications that he was deeply concerned about the security of his base, as the British had already made two commando-style attempts to damage the *Superior* during the course of her construction and one to sink her immediately after her launching. In the first instance, on the night of April 20–21, a single longboat had evaded the patrolling American boat pickets and landed a small party of men. Reaching the ship, they had intended to start a fire underneath her but, due to the patrolling guards, were detected and forced to withdraw before they were able to implement their plan. The second, more organized, attempt had taken place on the night of April 25–26, when three boats made an attempt to sneak into the basin — only to be detected, challenged, and fired upon by the boat pickets. As two of these boats were packed with barrels of black powder and rigged with fuses, their crews had wisely withdrawn to avoid being blown up and "hoist on their own petard." These deadly cargos were subsequently found by American patrols, abandoned a short distance up the lake. In addition, the third boat had also withdrawn, but interestingly had obviously been fitted for use as a diversion or separate attack, as it contained a launching frame for the firing of Congreve rockets from the deck of the boat and was manned by the Royal Marine artillery detachment. The final, and obviously desperate, attempt had taken place immediately after the launching, when a detachment of troops attempted to land on the night of May 2–3, but were unable to penetrate the harbour perimeter guards. After hiding throughout the day in the dense woods that lined the lake and being eaten alive by the even denser clouds of mosquitoes that infested the coastal underbrush, they had made a further attempt on the night of May 3–4, but were detected and forced to abandon the entire endeavour.

Looking to emerge with his newly strengthened fleet as soon as the *Superior* was fully fitted out, Chauncey had found the aforementioned overland transportation of the largest pieces, especially the cannon barrels, was impractical, given the state of the intervening roads. Consequently, he was forced to re-establish the use of boats (that would skirt the shores and move at night) to bring up these heavy supplies. However, he saw this solution temporarily thwarted when the larger vessels of Yeo's fleet, accompanied by a flotilla of gunboats, reappeared off the harbour on May 19th, thereby establishing a blockade of the intervening lakeside passage (the remaining vessels being dispatched in accordance with Yeo and Drummond's prior agreement to transport reinforcements and supplies up the lake to the Niagara frontier).

Suffering a recurrence of a previous illness that prevented his actively taking command of his fleet, Chauncey was equally determined not to see one of his subordinates gain a victory that should have been his to claim. He therefore ignored the calls from his captains to emerge with those ships already at his disposal in order to challenge the limited enemy squadron offshore. On the other hand, desperate to receive his armaments, Chauncey authorized Commandant Woolsey at Fredericksburg to make a convoy delivery by boats if any opportunity presented itself. This chance seemingly occurred on

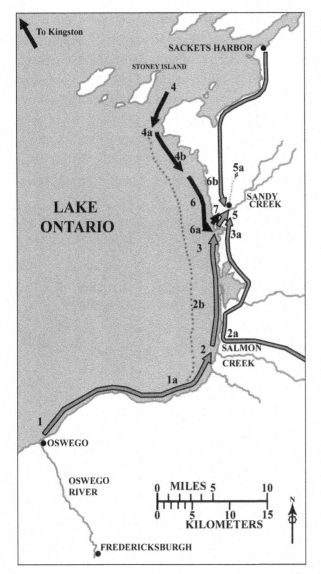

THE ENGAGEMENT AT SANDY CREEK, MAY 30, 1814

1. The American flotilla of boats (1) leaves Oswego under the cover of darkness on May 28, and sails east and then north along the shore of the lake (1a) toward Salmon Creek.
2. Arriving at Salmon Creek, shortly after dawn on May 29 (2), the Americans plan to layover in the creek to avoid detection and link up with their reinforcement guard of Allied Native warriors (2a). However, one boat is found to be missing (2b).
3. Worried that the missing boat will betray their mission, the flotilla presses on in daylight (3) to Sandy Creek, while the Native warriors move up the shoreline (3a).
4. Off Stoney Island, the British blockading squadron (4) sights the missing American boat to the south (4a) and intercepts it. Extorting the details of the American mission, two detachments of gunboats and bateaux are sent in pursuit (4b).
5. The American boats are manoeuvred deep into the winding course of Sandy Creek (5) and placed on the defensive in the stream. While detachments of the boat escort, boat crews, and Native warriors take up positions along the riverbank, a dispatch for reinforcements is sent post-haste to Sackets Harbor (5a).
6. As the British search the American shoreline (6) and make the fatal decision to enter Sandy Creek (6a), American reinforcements arrive (6b) from Sackets Harbor and take up positions along the riverbank.
7. The entire force of boats of the British force (7) enter Sandy Creek, fall into the American ambush, and are captured.

May 26th, when the British fleet was seen moving off station and up the lake. Dispatching immediate orders for the shipment to commence, Chauncey was later forced to send a message to abort when the enemy fleet reappeared. However, his countermand arrived too late, as the sixteen-boat convoy, under Woolsey, had already sailed on the 28th. Creeping up the Lake Ontario shoreline during the night, the convoy met up with a party of around 120 Oneida warriors, who were sent to act as an additional shore-based guard to supplement the 130 riflemen (Major Daniel Appling) onboard the boats. Unfortunately, some of the boats subsequently became separated in the darkness, with one falling into the hands of the re-established British blockade ships the following day (May 29th). Alerted to this American attempt, the British determined to intercept the rest of Woolsey's convoy by

(Top row) Details from the Storming of Oswego engraving shown above). Metro Toronto Reference Library, JRR-1171.

(Bottom row) Toronto Reference Library, T-16944 and T-16948.

Examples of the variety of vessels classified as gunboats and lost by the British at Sandy Creek.

dispatching a strong flotilla of three gunboats and four bateaux carrying over 200 sailors and Royal Marines (Captain Stephen Popham, R.N.) to locate and capture or destroy the enemy convoy.

Meanwhile, fearing the worst from the loss of the boat, Woolsey had taken refuge and set up a strong defensive position with his boats, well up the Sandy Creek waterway, some ten miles south of Sackets Harbor. He then notified Chauncey of his situation. In response, Chauncey had Brown send a detachment of troops that arrived the following day, only moments before Popham had ordered his flotilla (against Yeo's specific warnings) to enter the creek in pursuit — only to find itself manoeuvring upstream in ever-more restricted navigational conditions. As a result, Popham and his flotilla fell into the ambush laid by Woolsey. After losing eighteen killed and fifty wounded, and with his boats incapable of turning or retreating, Popham was forced to surrender his entire contingent. By this, not only did Yeo lose the boats, but also over 200 of his limited number of valuable ships crews and marines. Consequently, with this huge loss of manpower and shipping, Yeo felt he could no longer maintain the blockade and ordered the fleet return to Kingston, freeing the Americans to resume their building program. Yeo also made the decision that as the Americans would now be able to complete their super-frigates unimpeded, which would result in their ships outclassing the firepower of anything he had to counter with, his only option was to keep the bulk of his fleet safely in port till his own super ship, the *St. Lawrence*, was complete and able to help his fleet to take on the Americans. Even Lieutenant General Drummond saw the sense in this and backed Yeo's decision:

It appearing, however, from your [last] letter that the Enemy's squadron, including the new ship (*Superior*) and Brigs, is now ready for sea, it is evident the blockade has not had all the effect to which we looked, and moreover, that it can no longer be maintained, without risquing an action with a squadron quite equal, if not superior to that under your command, and under circumstances on our part of decided disadvantage.... It follows, therefore, ... that there exists at present no motive or object connected with the security of this Province which can make it necessary for you to act otherwise than cautiously on *the defensive* (but at the same time closely watching all their movements) until the moment arrives, when by the large Ship now on the stocks, you may bring the naval contest on this Lake fairly to issue,

or by a powerful combined expedition (if the Enemy, is as probable, should decline meeting you on the Lake) we may attack and destroy him in his stronghold.[3]
— Drummond to Yeo, June 6, 1813

The tide had fairly turned for the British and it was the Americans' turn to dictate the course of the naval conflict on Lake Ontario. Chauncey, although still ailing and reportedly becoming increasingly tetchy about *"his"* fleet and how it was to be deployed, did hold discussions with Major General Jacob Brown about future combined operations and mutually supporting activities — once the force at Buffalo was put into action and the main campaign on the Niagara began. Unfortunately, while Commodore Chauncey saw these discussions as nothing more than theoretical discussions of the two forces acting in an *equal* co-operation for their mutual benefit, Major General Brown took them as firm commitments of Yeo's agreement and verbal contract to act in *support* of Brown's army on the Niagara — especially as Brown now held the firm conviction that as the danger at Sackets Harbor had passed, it was time for him to leave and return to take up his position at the head of *his* army on the Niagara frontier. Although what he found upon his return may not have been the warm welcome he had been anticipating.

CHAPTER 7

Building a New Army

Following Major General Jacob Brown's departure from Buffalo for Sackets Harbor in April, the on-site disciplining and training of the American troops composing the Left Division was taken in hand under the personal direction of Brigadier General Winfield Scott. In later years, the heroic tale of Scott single-handedly whipping raw recruits into a disciplined fighting force by the use of a tattered drill book became the stuff of legend — most of it propagated by Scott himself. But more recent studies have shown that in reality, most of the troops and junior officers serving in this army at the time had already undergone considerable training and battlefield service during the previous eighteen months of war. What is beyond doubt,

Right: Major General Jacob Brown.

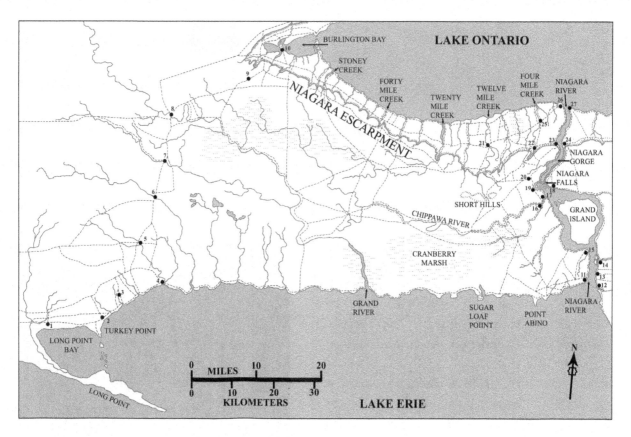

however, is that at no previous time had these troops been subject to the intensity and scope of training that was about to commence under the eagle eye of "Fuss and Feathers," Winfield Scott.

Day after day, for almost two months, the men of this new "model" army were put through every command in the established drill manual for up to ten hours each day. Commencing at the crack of dawn, company and section drills took up the mornings, while regimental and brigade manoeuvres consumed the afternoons and evenings, with only brief intervals to permit the men to rest and eat. Nor were the officers exempted from these rigours, as Scott pressed the point home that it was essential to create a military force that could fight a European army in a European

THE NIAGARA FRONTIER

Locations along the proposed American attack route from Long Point to Burlington Heights

1. Long Point (Port Rowan area)
2. Turkey Point
3. Dover (Port Dover)
4. Nanticoke
5. Union Mills (Simcoe)
6. Sovereign's Mills (Waterford)
7. Malcolm's Mill (Oakland)
8. Brantford
9. Ancaster
10. Burlington Heights

Locations along the actual American invasion route following the Niagara River

11. Fort Erie
12. Buffalo
13. Black Rock
14. Scajaquada Creek Navy Yard
15. Frenchman's Creek
16. Weishoun's Point
17. Chippawa Fortifications
18. Fort Schlosser
19. Bridgewater
20. Lundy's Lane/ Portage Road cross-road
21. Shipman's Corners (St. Catharines)
22. St. Davids
23. Queenston
24. Lewiston
25. Crossroads (Virgil)
26. Fort Mississauga/ Newark (Niagara-on-the-Lake)/Fort George
27. Fort Niagara

Brigadier General Winfield Scott.

manner and simultaneously undertake the difficulties of campaign without degenerating into an armed mob. Fundamental to this professional attitude was the strict enforcement of discipline, duties, and responsibilities upon both the officers and men — to the point where of twenty-six men held under arrest for various infractions nine were officers. Desertion was treated with the utmost rigor of military law, with the public execution of four out of five recaptured absconders serving as a stern reminder to the troops that the failures and deficiencies of the past were not going to be tolerated in the future. Nor was the vital aspect of health ignored. Remembering the winter horrors of sickness that had decimated the ranks at Sackets Harbor (when proper procedures for the disposal of sewage and waste were ignored), strict orders were issued for the establishment and maintenance of proper sanitary arrangements and regular cleaning of the living areas and camp kitchens — precautions that quickly reduced the incidents of sickness to a minimum. In addition, the troops were *ordered* to undertake the previously unheard of practice of regular bathing three times a week! Moreover, to ensure compliance with this directive, officers were directed to march their companies down to the lake and "cause the men to wash themselves from head to foot, but not to remain immersed in the water more than five minutes...."[1]

Over the following weeks, the men of the Left Division gradually became an efficient military force. Even their formidable commander expressed his approval of their state of training when he wrote, "I have a handsome little army.... The men are healthy, sober, cheerful and docile. The field officers highly respectable, and many of the platoon officers are decent and emulous of improvement. If,

of such material, I do not make the best army now in service, by the 1st of June, I will agree to be dismissed the service..."[2]

As the summer campaign season approached, additional regiments of regulars and militia arrived at Buffalo and were immediately subjected to the regimen of drills and manoeuvres in an attempt to bring them up to the standard being set by the original units of the corps.

We encamped on the left of the regulars in a piece of bushy ground, which was soon cleared off, making it a beautiful spot, with a fine spring close by the encampment. Regulations new to us and very strict were now adopted. We rose at 4 o'clock (reveille beat) and answered to our names. We had fifteen minutes to prepare for drill, which generally lasted one hour. Breakfast being over, the regiment was formed, roll again called, guards detailed, and the regiment dismissed for a short time.

The Sergeant's drill came next, which generally lasted till eleven o'clock. At two the Adjutant-General drilled, which was then dismissed till nine, when the roll was again called and we retired to rest. The time passed away in this manner, constant exercise, wholesome provisions, and strict discipline soon made our regiment have another appearance.[3]

— Alexander Mc Mullen,
Colonel Fenton's Regiment of
Pennsylvania Volunteers

Unfortunately, some elements of these militia reinforcements did not meet the exacting standards of Brigadier General Scott, and his opinions on these troops and their leadership became a significant source of friction within the American command structure in the ensuing campaign.

The [regular] troops here are getting into a state of very tolerable organization … & discipline. No exertions of mine have or shall be spared to perfect them in those essentials…. Col. Campbell & Com. Sinclair made a visit to Long Point a few days since; burned the mills & some other houses and have returned to Erie. No resistance of consequence was experienced. I now look for the fleet with the troops on board every hour. Col. Fenton & his militia are already in march for this place. I am sorry for this circumstance, for I had rather be without that species of force than have the whole population of New York and Pennsylvania at my heels. I now give it as my opinion that we shall be disgraced if we admit a militia force either into our camp or order of battle. By the way, I suspect Gov. Tomkins & P.B. Porter esqr. of a stratagem against myself & the other Brigadiers of this army. He [Porter] is very ingeniously styled General in all official communications between them; but whether he has the commission of Lieut. General or Maj. General in his pocket, is cautiously concealed. I wish not to conceal my determination never to submit to the orders of a militia-man whilst I hold a commission in the line. I hold myself prepared to leave the service on this point.[4]

— General Scott to General Brown,
May 23, 1814

As mentioned in Scott's letter, this new and largest of the American incursions into Upper Canada had taken place on May 14–16, when some 800 troops were transported by vessels from Erie, Pennsylvania, to the area around Long Point and Port Dover[*5] under Colonel John Campbell (Nineteenth Regiment). According to the local senior Canadian militia commander, Colonel Talbot:

... unfortunately, from the dispersed state of the Militia, it was impossible to assemble the Militia in sufficient time to oppose the landing of the Enemy.... The weather was so extremely foggy that the approach of the American vessels was not perceived more than an hour before they landed. I found it therefore necessary to retire as far as Sovereigns Mills, as did Lieu't Burton with the detachment of the 19th Light Dragoons, for the purpose of affording time for the Militia to collect.[6]

— Colonel Talbot to Drummond, May 16, 1814

ESTIMATE OF THE AMERICAN FORCE, RAID ON LONG POINT AREA, MAY 14–16, 1814[5]

Nineteenth Regiment (Captain Chunn), 1 company
Twenty-Second Regiment (Major Martin), amalgamated companies
Twenty-Fourth and Twenty-Seventh Regiment (Lieutenant Allison), amalgamated companies
Twenty-Sixth Regiment (Lieutenant McDonald), 1 company
Colonel Fenton's Pennsylvania Militia (Major Galloway and Major Wood), detachment
Canadian Volunteers (Abraham Markle), detachment
U.S. Sailors and Marines (Commander Unknown), artillery detachment, est. 50 men with three field pieces
Estimated total: approximately 800 all ranks

During the next two days, the communities at Patterson's Creek (Lynn River), Charlotteville (Turkey Point), Dover Mills, Finch's Mills, Long Point, and Port Dover all suffered from American attacks that saw the destruction of their public buildings, grain mills, distilleries, private homes, and barns at the hands of the invaders. Even the crops in the fields and cattle were deliberately destroyed in order to reduce the ability of the region to support the British Army in the field.

Without the support of the regular forces Drummond had previously planned to establish in this area to oppose exactly this kind of threat. The hastily assembled Canadian militia detachments and Light Dragoons could put up only a token show of opposition against the substantially larger landing force, backed by the guns of their ships. Nor could they keep up, as the Americans used their boats as rapid transports between their several landing points, whereas the infantry component of the defenders had to make a series of forced marches in their attempts to defend the various locations. Had the Americans now pressed home their advantage, or been properly supported by additional reinforcements as Brown had originally intended, there would have been nothing to stop them from marching overland, taking Burlington Heights, and cutting off the entire British force on the Niagara frontier. Instead, the Americans eventually retired from the region, leaving behind an area of scorched earth and smouldering buildings.

Less than a week later another American incursion, this time from the Detroit frontier, took place against Port Talbot. Composed of about thirty riflemen and guided by the renegade Andrew Westbrook, the American raiders entered the village with the intention of capturing Colonel Talbot and as many other militia officers as possible, as well as acquiring plunder and supplies. In the event, the colonel was at Long Point, dealing with the aftermath of Campbell's raid. However, the Americans did capture several other Canadian militia officers and men. Before they could retire with their prisoners and loot, however, it was learned that one of their prisoners had escaped. Alarmed that the escapee could guide any nearby Canadian militias or British regulars directly to their location or cut off their retreat, the Americans made a hasty departure with their loot and abandoned their prisoners — after forcing them to swear their paroles.

These two incursions so alarmed Major General Riall that despite having already abandoned the entire region of the upper Thames Valley, he now went so far as to request permission of Lieutenant General Drummond to withdraw most of his troops from their forward positions along the Niagara River and concentrate them at Burlington Heights, where, he argued, they could be used to counter any future American advance from the south, west, or east. Turning down this request, Lieutenant General Drummond ordered Riall to maintain his main force on the Niagara and strengthen his positions along the Grand River boundary as much as possible. By these measures, Drummond not only hoped to slow any possible American attack until reinforcements could be concentrated from their scattered positions elsewhere or brought up from York and Kingston, but was also determined to protect those inhabitants still attempting to scratch out a living and grow the crops that could feed his troops.

In addition, the fact that both raids had included renegade settlers persuaded the authorities to take a much harder line with those who were considered as turncoats and traitors and who came under the hand of the Crown. As a result, a group of nineteen Upper Canada residents who had gone over to the American side and then been captured while participating in earlier American raids, were arraigned on charges of high treason. A further fifty were charged in absentia. The trials for those in custody began in June at Ancaster and lasted for two weeks under the supervision of Chief Justice Thomas Scott, Senior Puisne Justice

William Powell, and Junior Puisne Justice William Campbell. Of those placed on trial, one pled guilty and four were acquitted. The remaining fourteen were found guilty and deemed subject to the penalty enacted on all those convicted of treason — death. In fact, only eight of this group were executed on July 8, 1814, while the remainder were reprieved and received varying terms of imprisonment. Three subsequently died of "jail fever," three were later pardoned, and one was reportedly able to escape his custody in the Kingston jail and succeeded in crossing into the United States.

Finally, these raids had another wider and long-term repercussion, as they resulted in yet another round of accusatory letters being dispatched; first from Major General Riall to Colonel Campbell on June 9th "to request from you an explicit declaration whether these acts were authorized by the Government of the United States."[7] To which Campbell proudly replied on June 16th, "I commanded the detachment … what was done at that place and its vicinity proceeded from my orders. The whole business was planned by myself and executed upon my own responsibility."[8] Riall also received testimonies from the victims of the raid that Campbell had repeatedly claimed the raid was a direct reprisal for the British burning of Buffalo the previous December. (For details see *The Flames of War.*)

This then brought in both Lieutenant General Drummond, who made an official complaint to Major General Brown at Buffalo, and Sir George Prevost, who made similar protestations to the American government about the depredations and wanton destruction committed on private property by Colonel Campbell's troops. In a remarkably short period of time, a court of inquiry was held at Buffalo under the superintendence of Brigadier General Winfield Scott, Major Thomas Jesup, and Major Eleazar Wood, who equally as rapidly exonerated Campbell of all imputation of wrongdoing in the burning of the mills, distilleries, sawmills, and associated structures (as in their judgement they were viable military targets, being used by the military to supply their needs). As to the burning of the private dwellings, Campbell was deemed to have been technically in error in those cases, but that the actions were understandable as a justified and honourable reaction to the prior unjustified and criminal British burning of civilian settlements at Buffalo. In a similar fashion, the American administration brushed off Prevost's complaint. This American aggression and the subsequent arrogant dismissal proved to be the final straw as far as Prevost was concerned and he subsequently dispatched highly incensed reports to both Whitehall and Vice Admiral Alexander Cochrane at Halifax, then commanding the British raiding forces operating along the American northeast coast. In this latter communiqué, Prevost indicated that, as far as he was concerned, if the Americans wanted to play a game of tit-for-tat in reprisals and burnings, Cochrane was free to show them what such a policy would result in — a reality that Stonington (CT), the settlements along the Chesapeake Bay, and ultimately Washington, D.C., felt during the forthcoming months.

CHAPTER 8

The Invasion of July 1814

Having returned to the Niagara frontier and resumed command on June 7, 1814, much to the displeasure of Brigadier General Scott, Major General Brown oversaw the final preparations for the upcoming invasion. Winfield Scott had seen to the training and discipline and now, finally, additional equipment and uniforms had arrived to outfit the soldiers. However, instead of the regulation high-collared blue coats with a short coattail, the shipment consisted of tailless grey jackets that were usually reserved for use as fatigue clothing or used as an extra layer in winter. Since there was no other supply of clothing available, the decision was made to redistribute the existing blue coats to the Twenty-First Regiment, while the remaining regiments were issued the grey jackets; a decision that would go down in military history and cause identification problems for the British in the days to come.

After the weeks of training and incessant drills, the men of the American Left Division were positively itching to go into action, and on July 2, 1814, they received their orders to commence the latest invasion of Canada. This was undoubtedly the best-trained fighting force the United States had fielded since the outbreak of the war.[*1]

Unfortunately, in later years the actual strength of this force became a matter of contention between several of the principal participants as they gave testimonies at the official inquiries and court martials dealing with the events that subsequently took place during this campaign. Many later American accounts used the figures marked with * in the sidebar in order to assess the initial

AMERICAN INVASION FORCE, JUNE 30, 1814[*1]

"Left Division" (Major General Brown)
First Brigade (Brigadier General Winfield Scott),
  Ninth Regiment: (Major Leavenworth), 16 officers, 332 other ranks* total: 642 all ranks,
Eleventh Regiment (Colonel Campbell), 17 officers,
  416 other ranks* total: 577 all ranks
Twenty-Second Regiment (Colonel Brady [absent]),
  12 officers, 217 other ranks* total: 287 all ranks
Twenty-Fifth Regiment (Major Jesup), 16 officers,
  354 other ranks* total: 619 all ranks
Total: 2,129 all ranks
Second Brigade (Brigadier General Ripley)
Twenty-First Regiment (Lieutenent Colonel Miller /
  Major Grafton), 25 officers, 651 other ranks*
  total: 917 all ranks
Twenty-Third Regiment (Major McFarland), 8 officers,
  341 other ranks* total: 496 all ranks
Total: 1,415 all ranks
Third Brigade (Brigadier General Porter)
Fifth Pennsylvania Militia Regiment (Major Wood),
  400–500 rank and file
New York Militia Regiments (Detachments)
Canadian Volunteers Regiment (Major Willcocks),
  830 all ranks
Artillery (Major Hindman)
Captain Towson's Battery, 101 all ranks
Captain Biddle's Battery, 104 all ranks
Captain Richie's Battery, 138 all ranks
Captain William's Battery, 73 all ranks
Total: 416 all ranks
Cavalry (Captain Harris)
Total: 1 Troop, 70–80 all ranks
Native Allies (Lieutenant Colonel Granger)
Total: 350–400 Warriors

size of the invasion force at around three thousand or less. Since this part of the official American regimental rolls only referred to those officers, non-commissioned officers, and rank and file actually present and on parade on the date given in the returns, it seriously underestimated the real size of the American invasion force, as it ignored all troops otherwise assigned for that day's guard pickets, camp duties and fatigues, detached duties away from the camp, and those reported as sick. In addition, it ignored all headquarters staff, commissariat and supply staff, musicians, pioneers, surgeons, etc. The total figures of the list do include these additional numbers, but make no breakdown by rank or service/duty. Since virtually all of these latter individuals would have been recalled from their designated duties to participate in the invasion, the actual invasion force entering Upper Canada should probably be assessed at somewhere around 5,000 men. This assessment is further supported by a letter that Brown forwarded to Secretary of War Armstrong on May 30, 1814, stating "General Porter has … from a thousand to twelve hundred [militia] engaged … if we are to be delayed until this force is in condition to act, much time will, I fear be wasted. With your approval I shall not hesitate to cross … with my four thousand Regulars, but it would no doubt be desirable to have a greater force, if a greater could be promptly assembled."[2] A similar letter followed on June 3rd, "I believe that from four to five hundred Native warriors may be induced to join us…. I shall consider it my duty to pass into the enemies country the moment I find at my command five thousand Regulars."[3] In return, Armstrong wrote to Brown on June 9th, "Sir … the difference between your effective strength and aggregate numbers is so great as to render it proper that you should immediately despatch an officer to call in and march to their regiments respectfully all absentees of the Line coming within the meaning of this order and are not, in any case, to be exempted from this order…."[4]

Irrespective of the actual numbers of troops involved in the invasion, there were a number of other inherent weaknesses in Brown's army that could not be explained away by playing with the statistics, and that would cause increasing degrees of problems during the upcoming campaign.

The first of these was Major General Brown's assumption that he had come to an understanding with Commodore Chauncey for the American naval force to emerge from Sackets Harbor and meet up with his army at Newark (Niagara-on-the-Lake) on or about July 10th. The fleet was intended to bring additional troops, supplies, and, most importantly, the heavy cannon needed to invest and take the fortifications of Fort Niagara and Fort George. Brown had based his entire strategy

on this rendezvous and was certain that Chauncey was preparing to move in concert with the invasion. Chauncey, on the other hand, had absolutely no intention of sailing until his new warships were fully ready and able to outgun Yeo's forces in any battle for control of the lake. Nor was he prepared to place *his* fleet at the convenience and timetable of any landsman general. As a result, Brown was effectively "on his own!"

Secondly, although he was the titular head of the Left Division, Major General Brown was still considered by some to be an amateur militiaman, and the old American bugbear of prejudice between regular and militia officers still existed, especially in the minds of Brown's supposed subordinates Scott and Ripley. Scott was of the decided opinion that since Brown had been essentially absent for much of the army's training, he (Scott) would naturally continue in command once it went into action. Thus, when Brown returned to take up his position in early June, Scott's nose was definitely put out of joint. Brigadier General Eleazar Ripley was, on the other hand, extremely dubious about the viability of the invasion plans once he was briefed, to the point that he requested a meeting with Brown to push for changes. When these were not forthcoming, he officially submitted his resignation on the eve of the invasion. While this was obviously a stinging vote of non-confidence against Brown's leadership, the senior

Brigadier General Eleazar Ripley.

Finally, although the Left Division was certainly the best-trained American army yet put into the field, it was the *only* such force that was available to Major General Brown, for no reserves or other forces of a similar quality were available to replace the inevitable losses that would occur once fighting began.

Surprisingly, up to this point the American administration had not issued any directives to Major General Brown about how the 1814 campaign was to be fought, despite the fact that, during his four months at Sackets Harbor, Brown had submitted several alternative plans. Directions did finally arrive at the beginning of June, but once again Secretary of War Armstrong's instructions and interference only succeeded in causing confusion and difficulties for his commanders in the field. In this latest communication, Armstrong applauded Brown's April proposal for an amphibious landing at Long Point, followed by a swift march overland to Burlington Heights to cut off Riall's forces in the peninsula. He also supported Brown's proposal that Chauncey should simultaneously break through the British blockade of Sackets Harbor with a cargo of supplies and reinforcements and rendezvous with Brown at Burlington Heights, prior to eliminating the trapped British troops on the Niagara frontier and effectively capturing Upper Canada in a single, bold stroke.

commander publically ignored the implications and simply refused to accept Ripley's resignation because it was not in the best interests of the nation. However, privately it left him bitter toward Ripley, thereafter causing him to question or disregard any advice and recommendations Ripley subsequently submitted. Consequently, Brown's leadership position and the degree to which he would be able to make command decisions during the campaign — without contradictory input from his brigade commanders — was compromised from the outset.

At the same time, however, while acknowledging that the proposed attack would require the use of every available ship on Lake Erie to land and then maintain the supply lines for any advance made by the army, Armstrong effectively crippled Brown's initiative by revealing that he had also ordered the repositioning of many of these same Lake Erie vessels to Detroit for use in a proposed attempt to recapture the fort at Michilimackinac (Mackinac) and secure the upper lakes for the Americans. To complete the confusion of his instructions, the secretary informed Major General Brown that while the amphibious assault was still to be considered the main attack, any implementation of it must wait for Commodore Chauncey to regain the dominant position on Lake Ontario. In the meantime, any delay could be used to the Americans' advantage as it would allow Ripley and Porter to move up to Buffalo and supplement Brown's forces with their own brigades in the overall invasion. Finally, in almost an afterthought, Armstrong proposed that since the troops already at Buffalo were ready, "To give ... immediate occupation to your troops & to prevent their blood from stagnating — Why not take Fort Erie & its garrison ... push forward a corps to seize the bridge at Chippawa, & be governed by circumstances in either stopping there, or going further...."[5] Thus, the single largest invasion of Upper Canada through the Niagara corridor

Brigadier General Peter B. Porter.

actually took place as the result of a hint on the part of the secretary of war as a measure to prevent Brown's troops becoming bored.

Unable to implement his earlier plan of attacking via Long Point, Major General Brown revised the route of the invasion to begin with a pincer movement on Fort Erie. Under this new scheme, a flanking force would cross the river at Black Rock. This attack was to be spearheaded by the First Brigade (Brigadier General Winfield Scott), followed immediately thereafter by part of the

Second Brigade (Brigadier General Eleazar Ripley). On the other flank, the remainder of the Second Brigade, the Third Brigade (Brigadier General Peter B. Porter), and Native Warrior allies were detailed to move out onto the lake and land further up the Canadian shoreline, before moving north to link up with the right wing, thus surrounding the fort.

Loading the waiting boats sometime after midnight, the leading elements pushed out into the Niagara River under the cover of a downpour of rain. Rowing hard against the current, the boats neared the far shore, only to be met with a volley from a small detachment of some twenty troops from the 100th Regiment stationed there. Undeterred by the immediate discovery of their intended landing, the boats pressed forward and, as soon as he deemed it viable, Winfield Scott swung himself over the side and into the water, determined to be the first to attack the enemy and lead his men by example from the very outset. Almost instantly the general disappeared below the water, only to reappear a moment later, drenched and spluttering; for although Winfield Scott was over six feet tall, he had made the mistake of disembarking directly over a deep pothole in the riverbed. In his subsequent memoirs he recalled the incident.

> ... sounding with [my] sword, [I] found the water less than knee deep, when personally leaping out, instead of giving the command — Follow Me! [I] Had scarcely time to exclaim — Too Deep! ... and ... had to swim for [my] ... life, ... It was a minute or two ... before the boat could be brought back to pick [me] up.[6]

For the men in the surrounding boats, who had endured weeks of backbreaking drills and undertaken the extraordinary (and possibly unwelcome) activity of regular bathing under the direct commands of this man, the sight of the general being well and truly dunked in that same cold water was possibly considered divine and sweet justice. What is certain is that these same soldiers knew better than to express their mirth while their commanding officer suffered the indignity of being hauled back into his boat like so much wet laundry. As the boats grounded on the shoreline, the first wave of men rushed forward into the darkness to establish a perimeter for the bridgehead. The British picket, inadequate to the duty of holding back this vastly superior force, retired on the fort to notify the garrison commander, Major Thomas Buck (8th [King's] Regiment), that the invasion had begun.

Placed at the end of the British defence perimeter and with a garrison of only 137 regular troops, plus a detachment of local Lincoln Embodied Militia, Major Buck was in the unenviable

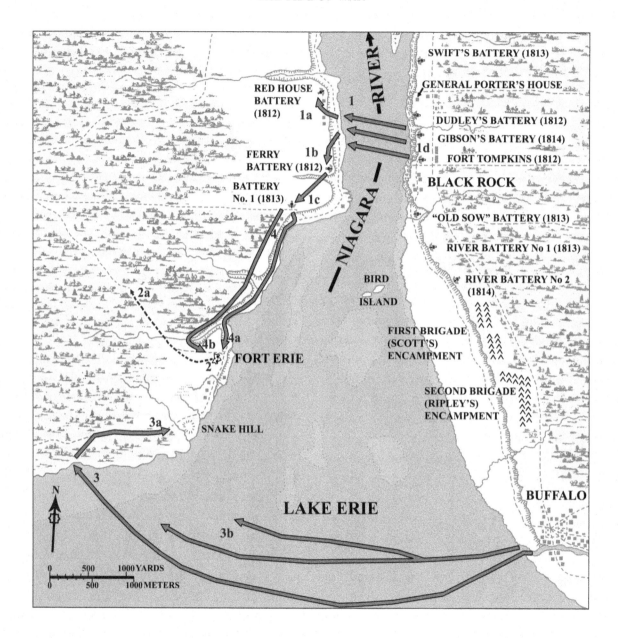

SWIFT'S BATTERY (1813)

GENERAL PORTER'S HOUSE

RED HOUSE
BATTERY
(1812)   1a

DUDLEY'S BATTERY (1812)

GIBSON'S BATTERY (1814)

1

RIVER

FERRY
BATTERY (1812)   1b

1d

FORT TOMPKINS (1812)

BATTERY
No. 1 (1813)   1c

BLACK ROCK

NIAGARA

"OLD SOW" BATTERY (1813)

RIVER BATTERY No 1 (1813)

4

RIVER BATTERY No 2
(1814)

2a

BIRD
ISLAND

FIRST BRIGADE
(SCOTT'S)
ENCAMPMENT

4b   4a

2   FORT ERIE

SECOND BRIGADE
(RIPLEY'S)
ENCAMPMENT

3a   SNAKE HILL

N

3

BUFFALO

LAKE ERIE

3b

0   500   1000 YARDS
0   500   1000 METERS

THE AMERICAN CROSSING AND INVASION OF JULY 3, 1814

1. In the pre-dawn of July 3, 1814, the leading wave of General Scott's First Brigade (1) make their crossing of the Niagara River and land downriver from Fort Erie after encountering only minimal resistance from the riverside picket guard. Establishing a beachhead, American detachments quickly overrun the nearby British shore batteries at the Red House (1a), the Ferry battery (1b), and battery No. 1 (1c). Additional waves of troops wait on the American shore for transport (1d).
2. At Fort Erie the garrison is alerted and prepares their defences (2) while sending dispatch riders (2a) with news of the American invasion to General Riall.
3. Due to delays in the transport of troops across the greater distance and open water of Lake Ontario, the initial wave of Ripley's pincer movement (3) is substantially delayed in reaching the Canadian shore and fails to arrive at Fort Erie as planned (3a), while subsequent waves encounter additional difficulties and delays (3b).
4. Without Ripley's support, Scott's force advances (4) on Fort Erie and establishes a partial encirclement (4a, 4b). Believing the situation makes it impossible to maintain any effective defence, Major Buck surrenders the position.

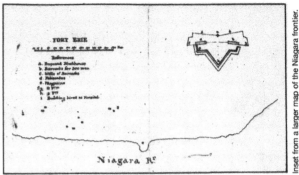

Fort Erie as it was intended to be repaired in the spring of 1814.

position of facing an unknown number of enemy that had already cut off his line of communication to his commander. Buck therefore decided to close the fort's gate and man the defences in hopes of holding out until Major General Riall could gather his forces and advance to meet the invader.[7] After shutting the gate, the men realized that no messenger had been sent to Riall to notify him of the situation. The obvious bearers for this communication were the few men of the 19th Light Dragoons, who had been specifically located at Fort Erie for this purpose. But the men's horses were in a stable outside the fort walls, and Buck was unwilling to reopen the gate lest the unseen Americans rush the fort. Instead, the troopers had to climb over the wooden palisade at the rear wall of the fort and drop into the muddy ditch below, before quietly finding their way to the stable and making their getaway with a warning for Major General Riall.

By dawn, most of the right wing of the American invasion force was ashore on the Canadian side of the river. However, the left wing

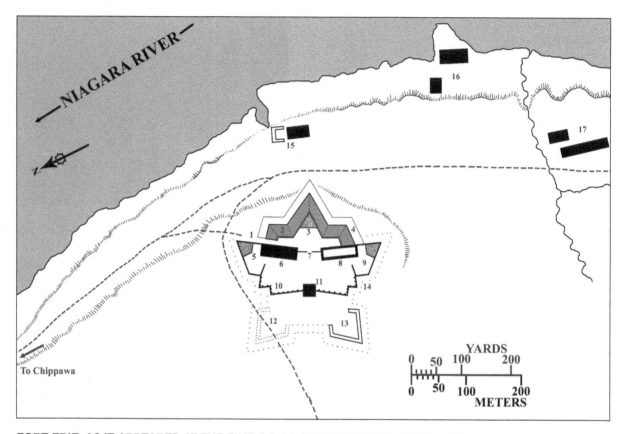

FORT ERIE, AS IT APPEARED AT THE TIME OF ITS SURRENDER ON JULY 3, 1814

1. Main entrance to the fort and outer gate
2. Eastern ravelin earthworks
3. Eastern ravelin artillery platform (designated for a 9-pounder gun)
4. Eastern ravelin ditch
5. Northeast bastion with artillery platform (designated for a 12-pounder gun)
6. Northeast two-storey stone mess house and barracks (partially repaired and roofed in)
7. Inner gate
8. Southeast two-storey mess house and barracks (burned-out shell and unroofed)
9. Southeast bastion with artillery platform (designated for a 12-pounder gun)
10. Western wooden picket wall
11. Western wall wooden blockhouse

12. Northwestern bastion foundation trace from pre-war period (no development construction work begun by this time)
13. Southwestern bastion foundation from the pre-war period (only consisting of a partial stone foundation rising to ground level)
14. Pre-war partially excavated and trace line of proposed ditch
15. Derelict lime-kiln foundation and small warehouse building
16. and 17. Civilian and military warehouses

was still in the process of crossing. Unwilling to wait, Scott advanced toward Fort Erie with only the Twenty-Fifth Regiment. In response, the guns and muskets of the fort opened fire, inflicting several casualties on the detachment surrounding the Twenty-Fifth's regimental colours[8] but with little other overall effect. Major Buck was facing hopeless odds, without possibility of relief for at least one or two days. Conferring with his fellow officers, some called for a to-the-last-man! defence of the fort, but the majority opinion was that surrender was inevitable and the best course was to avoid unnecessary casualties. To this end, Buck sent out a flag of truce and entered into negotiations for

The reconstructed and restored interior courtyard of the historic Fort Erie complex in 2013. The Northwest mess house and interior gate stand to the right. The earthworks and artillery platform on the left were part of the substantial alterations made by the Americans later in 1814.

BRITISH FORCES, "RIGHT DIVISION,"
JUNE 22, 1814[7]

Fort Niagara (Lieutenant Colonel Hamilton, 100th Regiment)

Staff	21 officers
Royal Artillery	1 officer, 12 other ranks
Royal Marine Artillery	2 officers, 33 other ranks
8th (King's) Regiment	1 other ranks
100th Regiment	23 officers, 21 drummers, 568 other ranks, 25 other ranks sick

Total: 47 officers, 21 drummers, 614 other ranks, 25 other ranks sick

Fort George and Fort Mississauga (Lieutenant Colonel Gordon, 1st [Royal Scots] Regiment)

19th Light Dragoons	2 officers, 1 bugler, 30 other ranks, 5 other ranks sick
Provincial Light Dragoons	2 officers, 19 other ranks
Royal Engineers	1 officer
Royal Artillery	2 officers, 2 buglers, 19 other ranks, 5 other ranks sick
Royal Artillery Drivers	3 other ranks, 4 other ranks sick
Royal Marine Artillery	3 officers, 1 bugler, 34 other ranks
Incorporated Militia Artillery	4 other ranks
1st (Royal Scots) Regiment	23 officers, 18 drummers, 721 other ranks, 88 other ranks sick
103rd Regiment	4 officers, 1 drummer, 135 other ranks
Coloured Corps	1 officer, 22 other ranks

Total: 38 officers, 23 drummers/buglers, 987 other ranks, 102 other ranks sick

Queenston (Major Deane, 1st [Royal Scots] Regiment)

19th Light Dragoons	9 other ranks
Royal Artillery	40 other ranks
Royal Artillery Drivers	1 bugler, 18 other ranks
1st (Royal Scots) Regiment	10 officers, 4 drummers, 208 other ranks, 8 other ranks sick

Total: 10 officers, 5 drummers/buglers, 275 other ranks, 8 other ranks sick

Chippawa (Colonel Young, 8th [King's] Regiment)

19th Light Dragoons	5 other ranks
Royal Artillery	11 other ranks
Incorporated Militia Artillery	8 other ranks
Royal Artillery Drivers	7 other ranks
8th (King's) Regiment	25 officers, 8 drummers, 426 other ranks, 8 other ranks sick
Native allies (John Norton)	300 warriors

Total: 25 officers, 8 drummers, 441 other ranks, 8 other ranks sick, 300 warriors

Fort Erie (Major Buck, 8th [King's] Regiment)

19th Light Dragoons	1 officer, 24 other ranks
Royal Artillery	12 other ranks
8th (King's) Regiment	8 officers, 1 drummer, 118 other ranks

Total: 9 officers, 1 drummer, 154 other ranks

Long Point (Lieutenant Colonel Parry, 103rd Regiment)

19th Light Dragoons	3 officers, 1 bugler, 59 other ranks
Provincial Light Dragoons	1 officer, 14 other ranks
89th Regiment	1 other rank sick
103rd Regiment	11 officers, 2 drummers, 200 other ranks
Loyal Kent Volunteer Militia	3 officers, 44 other ranks

Total: 18 officers, 3 Drummers, 272 other ranks, 6 other ranks

Burlington Heights (Colonel Hercules Scott, 103rd Regiment)

Provincial Light Dragoons	3 other ranks
Royal Artillery	1 officer, 18 other ranks, 1 other ranks sick
Royal Artillery Drivers	1 officer, 16 other ranks
1st (Royal Scots) Regiment	1 other rank sick
89th Regiment	1 other rank sick
103rd Regiment	18 officers, 20 drummers,379 other ranks, 20 other ranks sick

Total: 20 officers, 20 drummers, 416 other ranks, 23 other ranks sick

York (Colonel Stewart, 1st [Royal Scots] Regiment)

Royal Artillery	12 other ranks
Royal Artillery Drivers	1 officer, 10 other ranks

Royal and Provincial Engineers	2 officers, 18 other ranks
1st (Royal Scots) Regiment	2 officers, 4 other ranks, 4 other sick
8th (King's) Regiment	4 other ranks
41st Regiment	29 officers, 17 drummers, 526 other ranks, 12 other ranks sick
Royal Newfoundland Regiment	1 officer, 1 other rank, 1 other rank sick
Incorporated Militia Regiment	29 officers, 11 drummers, 366 other ranks, 25 other ranks sick

Total: 64 officers, 28 drummers, 969 other ranks, 42 other ranks sick

the surrender of the garrison. Around 5:00 p.m. Buck's force marched out into captivity,[9] while American musicians played "Yankee Doodle" and Captain George Howard's company of the Twenty-Fifth U.S. Infantry Regiment entered the fort and raised their country's flag as a sign of ownership by its new occupants.

Receiving word of the American invasion around 8:00 a.m. on July 3rd, Major General Riall immediately ordered five companies of the 1st (Royal Scots) Regiment, stationed at Fort George, to march on the Chippawa defence lines and soon followed with his staff to personally assess the

AMERICAN CASUALTIES, CAPTURE OF FORT ERIE, JULY 3, 1814[18]

Twenty-Fifth Regiment
Killed   1 sergeant, 10 rank and file
Wounded   2 sergeants, 1 musician, 10 rank and file

BRITISH TROOPS SURRENDERED AT FORT ERIE, JULY 3, 1814[19]

8th (King's) Regiment	1 officer (Major)
Royal Artillery	1 officer (Lieutenant), 21 gunners
100th Regiment	4 officers (1 Captain, 2 Lieutenants, 1 Ensign) 4 sergeants, 3 musicians, 101 rank and file

situation. At Chippawa the commanding officer, Lieutenant Colonel Thomas Pearson (previously the commander of Fort Wellington at Prescott and a senior officer at the Battle of Crysler's Farm, for details see *The Flames of War*), had maintained the alert with his garrison since the cavalrymen had passed through during the night, and was subsequently joined by around 300 Native Warriors later in the day. Unfortunately, this supposed reinforcement was somewhat less than reliable, for while it was officially under the leadership of John Norton, it was, in fact, composed of a set of competing factions, due to a political power struggle that had taken place during the winter between Norton and the older (and likely corrupt) Native Department liaison officer, William Claus. Claus had been a person of power amongst the Native tribes before the war but had strongly resented his authority being undermined by the younger and more aggressive Norton as the war progressed. Consequently, Claus took every opportunity to undermine Norton's authority and leadership, while openly ignoring the orders of generals Drummond and Prevost to support Norton's Native recruiting activities for the British cause.

Despite the potential unreliability of his allies, Pearson led a strong reconnaissance force toward Fort Erie in order to gain better intelligence of the enemy's dispositions, strength, and possible intentions. Reaching the area of the ferry dock opposite Black Rock, Pearson noted the rapid build-up of enemy troops and artillery around the fort. In addition, local residents passed rumours of additional American landings at Point Albino and troops massing on Grand Island for a possible assault on Chippawa. Retiring to the Chippawa River, Pearson left pickets behind to maintain contact with the enemy and report on their movements. By the evening of July 3, 1814, most of the American invasion force was on the west bank of the river and preparing to move north in the morning. At the same time, Riall and Pearson were busily engaged in improving the strong defensive position along the north bank of the Chippawa River by constructing additional earthworks and manning them with the various companies of troops that arrived as the day progressed. Although the Chippawa line gave Major General Riall his best hope of stopping the Americans, he realized he needed to slow down any American advance in order to complete his defences. He also erroneously believed that Fort Erie was still holding out and that most of the American force would be occupied in forcing its surrender, leaving him the possible opportunity of making a rapid counterattack if only a part of the American army advanced on Chippawa. Consequently, Lieutenant Colonel Pearson was ordered to march a strong detachment forward during the night and delay the Americans as much as possible should they advance from Fort Erie.

The following morning (July 4th), the American Army began the day by celebrating their national holiday with a round of volleys. Further celebrations would have to wait, however, as Major General Brown directed Winfield Scott's brigade to advance toward Chippawa, supported by units of artillery and cavalry.

Marching out from their camp, the First Brigade had only advanced about four miles (6

The route of Lieutenant Colonel Thomas Pearson's delaying retreat of Brigadier General Winfield Scott's Brigade from Fort Erie to Chippawa, July 4, 1814.

kilometers) north when it came upon Pearson's force drawn up on the far bank of Putnam's Creek, where it entered the Niagara River. Swollen by heavy rains that had fallen during the past several days, the only way to cross the turbulent creek was over a small wooden bridge that the British had partially demolished by tearing up the wooden roadbed. Faced by a force of infantry, artillery, and cavalry, Winfield Scott applied the lessons he had drilled into his troops by changing the brigade formation from column into line-of-battle. True to their training, the various units swung out smartly and took up their positions, ready to commence the attack. However, instead of immediately engaging the enemy, the vastly more experienced Pearson patiently watched and waited as the Americans took the time to complete their manoeuvres and then simply had his artillery and infantry fire a single volley at the deployed Americans before marching off, leaving Winfield Scott and his troops looking at an empty field.

Forced to take additional time to replace the wooden planking of the bridge, Winfield Scott reformed his columns and impatiently awaited the completion of the repairs before recommencing his advance; only to find that Pearson had simply retired three miles (5 kilometers) before redeploying his force on the north bank of the flooded Frenchman's Creek. Once again the sequence of American deployment, British volley, British retirement, and American repair of the bridge were enacted. Nor did it stop there; as the day wore on, Pearson repeated this delaying tactic at each and every creek, infuriating Scott, who was keen to come to grips with the enemy. By the time the

Americans had reached Black's Creek their desire to fight had outstripped their caution, and a company of the Ninth Regiment (Captain Crooker) saw an opportunity to threaten the British artillery as it commenced limbering up its guns. Pressing forward on the American left flank, the men of Crooker's company waded through the deep water and advanced on the guns through a belt of trees. Unfortunately, what Crooker failed to note was the troop of experienced cavalrymen of the 19th Light Dragoons (Lieutenant Horton) covering the British withdrawal. Emerging into the open from the woods, the Americans saw, to their alarm, that instead of facing exposed artillery, a detachment of enemy cavalry was rapidly bearing down on them. Under perfect circumstances, the theoretical defence of infantry in line against attacking cavalry would be to "form square," while an extended line of skirmishers would seek the cover of the nearest physical obstacle to prevent the cavalry running them down. In reality, the usual response of even the best infantry caught in the open and faced with the sight of charging cavalry is to run like h**l. To the credit of Captain Crooker and his men, the company did not break and run; instead it fired a volley at the approaching cavalry before racing toward a nearby farmhouse. This volley hit several of the cavalrymen and the charge faltered, allowing Crooker and his men time to reach the building. From this cover, the infantry engaged the cavalry on far better terms and, after some ineffectual exchanges of gunfire, the British cavalry withdrew once they saw that their guns had been safely withdrawn.

Now no impediment to the American advance remained, except the Chippawa River and its defences. But Pearson's delaying tactics had used up the bulk of the day and it was near sunset when the American column approached the small hamlet of Chippawa. Once the last of the British rearguard crossed the Chippawa bridge, the centre spans of the roadbed were torn up, making the structure impassable. At a width of over two hundred feet (61 meters) and some twenty feet (6 meters) deep at its mouth, the Chippawa River was well chosen as the primary line of British defence. To prevent the Americans gaining any sort of cover near the bridge, Major General Riall was also forced to order the burning of those houses on the south bank that had survived the depredations of war since 1812. Under the pall of smoke from the burning buildings and a torrential downpour of rain, Winfield Scott's brigade approached the riverbank, only to be met with a heavy fire from the British artillery batteries on the opposite shore. Recognizing that nothing more could be achieved that day, and knowing his men were exhausted from their daylong march,

Chippawa Village, Sempronius Stretton, artist, 1804. The view looking south across the Chippawa River bridge toward the small village of Chippawa in 1804. Neither the bridge, nor buildings, survived the war intact.

Scott marched his troops back some two miles (5 kilometers), to a position alongside Street's Creek. Here he established his camp and decided to await the arrival of Major General Brown with the remainder of the army before tackling the significant barrier of the Chippawa and its defences. After midnight, Ripley's second brigade finally arrived. Too tired to erect tents, the men simply lay on the sodden ground for the remainder of the night, perhaps thinking that this was no way to pass a national holiday.

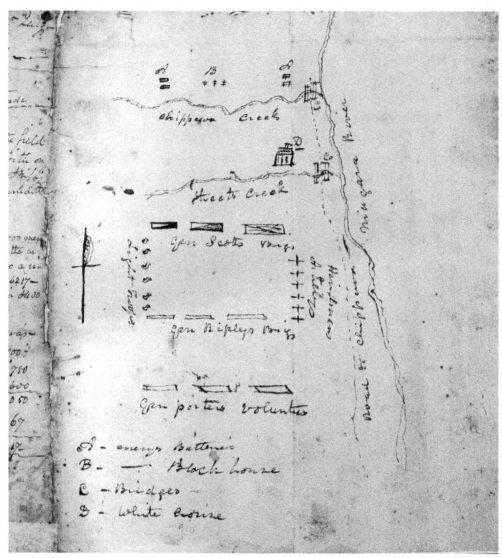

A page from a contemporary notebook, containing numerous valuable details about the 1814 American campaign on the Niagara, including this drawing of the layout of the American encampment at Chippawa in July 1814.

CHAPTER 9

The Battle of Chippawa

For Major General Riall, the American landing at Fort Erie triggered a preplanned concentration of his troops from as far away as York and Burlington into the Niagara frontier, while the units at Queenston and Fort George bolstered the Chippawa River defence line. Confident of the strength of this defensive position, Riall was well pleased with the delaying tactics of Lieutenant Colonel Pearson, while the support of the Native Natives gave him an additional light force to harass the enemy flanks. By the morning of July 5, further units of regular and militia infantry, artillery and cavalry had arrived to bolster his line.[*1] His choice now was whether to remain on the defensive or to attack.

Because he had developed a low opinion of the quality of the American troops after their dismal

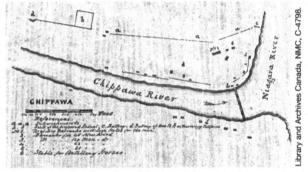

A pre-war map of the military positions and bridge at the mouth of the Chippawa (now Welland) River. Inset from a larger map of the Niagara frontier.

showing at Buffalo the previous December (for details see *The Flames of War*), and having made his own reconnaissance of the American positions that persuaded him that Fort Erie was detaining a sizeable part of the American force at the far end of

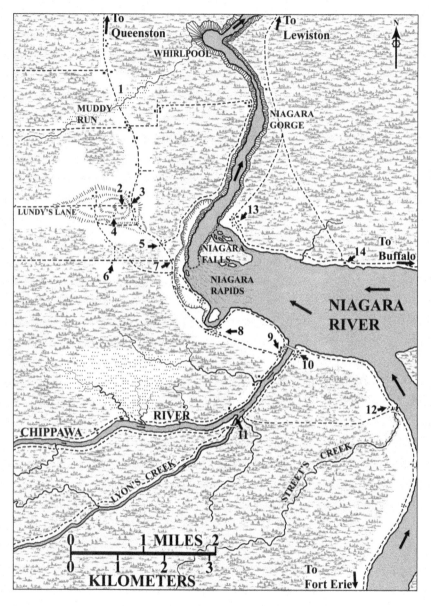

LOCATIONS AROUND THE GREAT FALLS OF NIAGARA JULY, 1814

1. Cook's bog or "muddy run"
2. The Lundy's Lane church on the hilltop
3. Johnson's Tavern at the Lundy's Lane/Portage Road crossroad
4. Buchner farmstead
5. Forsyth's Tavern
6. Haggai Skinner's farmstead
7. Mrs. Wilson's tavern
8. Bridgewater Mills
9. British fortifications at the Chippawa River
10. Chippawa Village
11. Weishoun's Point
12. Ussher's farmstead

BRITISH FORCES, BATTLE OF CHIPPAWA, JULY 5, 1814[*1]

(Major General Phineas Riall)

British Regulars

1st (Royal Scots) Regiment (Lieutenant Colonel John Gordon), 500 rank and file
8th (King's) Regiment (Major Thomas Evans), 480 rank and file
100th Regiment (Lieutenant Colonel George Hay, Marquis of Tweedale), 450 rank and file

Canadian Militia

2nd Lincoln Militia Regiment (Lieutenant Colonel Thomas Dickson), 200 rank and file
Artillery (Captain James Maconochie)
Lieutenant Sheppard's Battery (3 x 6-pounder guns)
Lieutenant Armstrong's Battery (2 x 24-pounder guns)
Lieutenant Jack's Battery (1 x 5 ½ inch Howitzer)
Total: 70 crew
Cavalry (Major Robert Lisle)
19th Light Dragoons, 70 troopers
British Native Allies (Captain Norton)
300–350 Warriors

AMERICAN FORCES, BATTLE OF CHIPPAWA, JULY 5, 1814[*2]

(Major General Jacob Brown)
First Brigade (Brigadier General Winfield Scott)

Ninth/Twenty-Second Regiment (Major Henry Leavenworth), 700 rank and file
Eleventh Regiment (Major John McNeil), 500 rank and file
Twenty-Fifth Regiment (Major Thomas Jesup), 360 rank and file
Second Brigade (Brigadier General Eleazar Ripley)
Nineteenth/Twenty-First Regiment (Major Joseph Grafton) 725 rank and file (80, Ropes' Coy)
Twenty-Third Regiment (Major Daniel McFarland), 450 rank and file
Third Brigade (Brigadier General Peter B. Porter)
Fifth Pennsylvania Militia Regiment (Major James Wood), 540 rank and file (200)
American Native Allies (Lieutenant Colonel Erastus Granger), 400 Warriors (300)
Artillery (Major Jacob Hindman)
Captain Biddle's Battery (3 x 12-pounder guns, 80 crew) (25)
Captain Richie's Battery (3 x 6-pounder guns and one 5 ½ inch howitzer, 96 crew) (96)
Captain Towson's Battery (2 x 6-pounder guns and one 5 ½ inch howitzer, 89 crew) (89)
Captain William's Battery (3 x 18-pounder guns, 62 crew)
Cavalry (Captain Samuel D. Harris)
Light Dragoons (1 troop)

(*N.B.* Although these figures represent what was at the field during the day, only portions of the Second and Third brigades saw action. The bracketed figures are an estimate of the real numbers of American rank and file that fought on the day and, as in the case of the British figures, do not include non-commissioned officers, officers, command staff, and supporting forces.)

the Niagara River, Riall believed there was an opportunity to strike at the enemy while they were still separated. He therefore decided to advance and attack the American encampment. What he didn't know was that as well as Ripley's Second Brigade, Porter's Third Brigade had now completed its crossing of the Niagara River and was advancing north to create an American force that far outnumbered Riall's own.[*2]

Prior to this fateful decision, Riall had sent out his Native allied troops during the night with orders to skirt the American encampment and scout out their dispositions, but not engage the enemy. While Norton's warriors obeyed this directive, some of those refusing to obey Norton's leadership found the American sentries too much of a tempting target and began firing, inevitably drawing fire in return. Initially ignoring the harassing fire, Major General Brown's patience had worn thin by noon and he chose to use Porter's approaching column of militia and American Native allies to clear the woods of this annoyance. According to General Porter's later account, General Brown notified him that:

> … about three fourths of a mile distance between the river and an almost impenetrable forest was infested with a band of Indians & militia conversant with its haunts & sent from the British camp to

The Opening Moves, 5:00 a.m–3:30 p.m.

A Chippawa fortifications and main British lines
B Chippawa Village
C Ussher's farmstead, location of U.S. advance post guarding the Street's Creek Bridge
D Brigadier General Scott's (First Brigade) encampment
E Brigadier General Ripley's (Second Brigade) encampment

1. In the morning, British Native allies (1) engage in reconnaissance (1a) of the American positions. However, against orders some warriors (1b) fire upon the American encampment picket guards (1c–1d).
2. Around noon, Brigadier General Porter's Third Division (2) arrives from Fort Erie and begin clearing the woods of the enemy force (1b). The assigned units create an extended cordon (2a–2b) before advancing north (2c) in search of the enemy at around 3:00 p.m.
3. Major General Riall, mistakenly believing the American forces are still separated, orders an advance to attack the American encampment at around 3:00 p.m. The advance consists of the combined light companies of the 1st (Royal Scots), 8th (King's), 100th, 2nd Lincoln Militia Regiment, and British Native allies (hereafter light troops) (3). The main column is the 19th Light Dragoons (3a), the 100th Regiment (3b), Armstrong's artillery battery (3c), Sheppard's artillery battery (3d), the 1st (Royal Scots) Regiment (3e), and 8th (King's) Regiment (3f). A separate detachment of Native allies (under Norton) (3g) moves off to flank the American positions.

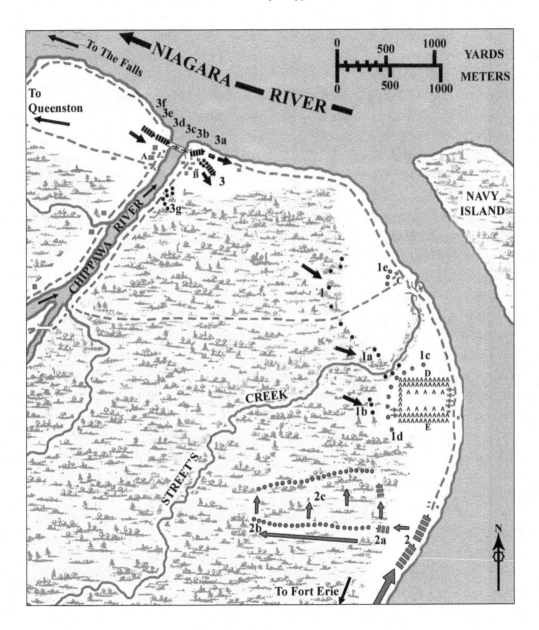

annoy and assail our pickets; that he had that morning been under the necessity of making an example of a valuable officer [Captain Treat (Twenty-First Regiment)] for suffering his guard to be driven in [and leaving a wounded man on the field] & the army thus exposed to the direct fire of these troublesome visitants. That it was absolutely necessary for their quiet & safety of the camp that these intruders should be dispersed; and as regular troops were ill qualified for such service ... that he [Porter] should with his Corps of warriors, aided if necessary by the volunteers, scour the adjoining woods and drive the enemy across the Chippawa, handling them in such a manner as would prevent a renewal of this kind of warfare — assuring him in the most confident terms that there was not and would not be in the course of that day, a single regular British soldier on the south side of the Chippawa.[3]

Coincidentally, this was just about the time Major General Riall ordered his troops to repair the Chippawa bridge and prepare for an attack. Because a wide band of trees blocked the line of sight between the open ground of the Chippawa riverbank and the fields in front of the American camp, neither general was fully aware of the movements of their enemy. Consequently, when they both decided to advance their light troops through the woods to the west of the American camp, a collision of forces became inevitable.

Having just marched from Fort Erie under hot and humid conditions, Porter's men were tired. Nevertheless, more than 200 of the Pennsylvania Militia volunteered to participate in the attack. Giving these men time to take a brief rest and eat, Porter also detailed his 300 Native warriors to join in the advance. Preparing for battle, Porter's warriors applied war paint and tied strips of white cloth around their heads to distinguish them from the warriors fighting for the British.

Around 3:30 p.m. both forces began to move out from their respective encampments. From the British positions, Riall led his force across the repaired bridge. Leading the advance was a strong detachment, composed of the light companies of the 1st (Royal Scots), 8th (King's), 100th, 2nd Lincoln Militia regiments, and a body of Native warriors (who had refused to follow Norton). After crossing the river, this force was detached to the right, where it halted and fronted the woods, anchoring the British line of advance. Meanwhile, the main body of troops (the 19th Light Dragoons, the remaining companies of the 100th regiment, the artillery batteries of Lieutenant Armstrong and Lieutenant Sheppard, the remaining companies of the 1st [Royal Scots] regiment, and the remaining companies of the 8th [King's] regiment), followed the curve of the track that paralleled the Niagara River, marching toward the American camp. In addition, a separate body of Native allies under Norton crossed over and advanced further to the right (west), intending to outflank the American pickets and come at the American camp from the rear.

For their own part, Porter's Native warriors, Pennsylvanian volunteers, and a detachment from the regulars under Ripley's Aide (Lieutenant McDonald) advanced up to the wood line, with the Native warriors passing into the woods in single file, while the militia and regulars remained in the open ground, thus creating a cordon of men that stretched for almost three-quarters of a mile (one kilometer). Upon command, this line then halted, faced to the right (north), and began to cautiously sweep forward through the dense bush toward Street's Creek and the sounds of the sporadic firing of the enemy upon the American camp. Within moments, the Americans began to encounter small parties of British allied Natives. Outflanked and outnumbered, many wisely took to their heels and attempted to outrun the advancing wave of Americans, while others, finding themselves cut off, fought until they were overwhelmed, with no quarter being given on either side. Within a short

time, the American advance had degenerated into clusters of men engaged in a running battle, with visibility restricted to a few yards and hand-to-hand combat being the rule. Outside the woods, Major General Brown rode north and was able to follow the advance of Porter's troops by listening to the sporadic sounds of musket fire coming from the treeline. By the time he reached Brigadier General Scott's camp, things seemed to be going well, as the harassing fire on the sentries had ceased and was receding further north toward the British position at the Chippawa. Having promised Porter the tactical support of Winfield Scott's troops should it be necessary, and finding Scott was asleep in his tent, Brown deduced this would not be required and continued forward to the advanced picket lines on the far side of Street's Creek. Suddenly, the sounds of firing from the woods changed dramatically, for instead of the staccato and overlapping fire of individual muskets, the noise deepened into the rumbling barks that could only be produced by musket volleys from disciplined troops, formed in line-of-battle.

This sonic signal, indicating that the fighting had entered a new and more serious phase, was the result of a series of events that had taken place unseen by Brown, during the previous half hour. Within the woods the rout of the British Natives had led the American Natives forward at such an impetuous pace they were unprepared for what lay ahead as they approached the northern limit of the woods. For his part, Lieutenant Colonel Pearson, commanding the British light troops, militia, and part of the Native force, noted the approaching noises of firing from the woods to his front and advanced the 2nd Lincoln Militia Regiment, supported by a force of one hundred western Native warriors, into the woods to counter the obvious American advance. As a result, the two forces met head-on in the dense woods and a firefight ensued, in which the American Native allies fared worse and began to retire in as much haste as they had previously advanced. Moving forward in their turn, the Lincolns and British Native allies came up against more and more American warriors who were by then rallying alongside the position of the American Third Brigade militiamen and the reserve of regulars. The two forces began to fire into each other at extremely close range, inflicting casualties on both sides. After some fifteen minutes of intense fighting, the Lincolns and Natives pulled back once more and emerged from the woods, hotly pursued by the entire body of Americans, who were intent on catching their enemy — that is, until they suddenly burst out from the forest into the open ground and realized that instead of chasing militia and Natives they were facing a solid wall of redcoats in line.

The British regulars and regrouped militiamen opened up on the surprised Americans with their disciplined volleys (thus alerting Brown at the American camp that a new element had been added to the day's conflict) before advancing with the bayonet into the woods, sweeping all before them. This time there was no hope of Porter rallying his forces and the American general joined his men in retiring back toward the American camp with all dispatch.

Meanwhile, Major General Riall had marched his main force of regulars along the dusty riverside road and past a belt of trees that almost reached to the riverbank, before ordering the 1st (Royal Scots) and 8th (King's) regiments to move off to the right into more open ground. As a result, the British force now advanced in three separate columns, placed in echelon. Opposite him, Major General Brown reacted to the sounds of volley fire and the approaching dust clouds by dispatching his adjutant general, Colonel Gardner, to order the First Brigade forward and then bring up the Second Brigade in support. Reaching Winfield Scott's tent, Gardner found the general awake and in a good mood after his nap, while his troops were "kitting up" and forming their companies. To Gardner's concern, however, he learned that, far from preparing to go into battle, the men of the First Brigade were dressing to practise drill manoeuvres according to Scott's orders for the day. Attempting to

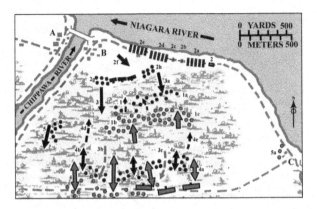

The Fight in the Forest, 3:30–3:50 p.m.

A Chippawa fortifications and main British lines
B Chippawa Village
C Ussher's Farmstead, location of U.S. advance post guarding the Street's Creek Bridge

1. British Native allies (1–1a), faced with the advance of the strong force of American militia and Native allies (1b–1c), retreat toward Chippawa village (B).
2. The main British column (2–2e) advances along the riverbank road, as the light troops (2f) move up to the wood line and form a line (2g–2h) in response to the approaching sounds of firing within the forest.
3. Detachments of the Canadian militia and British Native allies (3, 3a) advance to support the retreating British Native allies (1, 1a) and force the leading elements of the advancing Americans (1b, 1c) to retreat (3b–3c).
4. Accumulating reinforcements from their own forces, the American's rally (4–4a) and counterattack the advancing British (4b–4c), forcing the British to retreat (4d–4e) toward their supporting line (2g–2h).
5. Norton's warriors (5) continue their flanking movement through the forest, while at Ussher's farmstead (C) near the riverbank, Captain Ropes' company of the Twenty-First Regiment (5a) is alerted to possible British movements by the clouds of dust approaching from Chippawa.

alert the general to the imminent danger, Colonel Gardner was dismissed by Scott as an alarmist. Nevertheless, Scott obeyed his new orders and led his brigade toward Street's Creek, where he met up with Major General Brown, who was returning in haste to form his army, having already seen the columns of redcoats emerging from the woods to the north. Even now, Scott discounted Brown's admonition that he was going into battle and retorted with his positive conviction that "he would march and drill his Brigade but that he did not believe he should find 300 of the enemy...."[4] He then self-confidently marched his brigade past a wall of bushes and trees lining the creek and reached the cleared ground alongside the bridge. At this moment, Scott's arrogant illusions were quickly swept away as the advancing British troops came into his view and Armstrong's artillery battery opened fire upon his brigade.

Leading the British force of some 1,200 rank and file onto the field, Major General Riall ordered his columns to deploy into line across the open ground. Nearest the Niagara River and anchoring

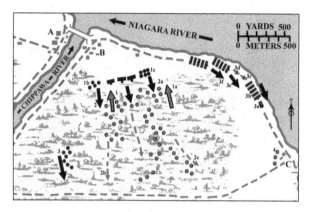

The American Third Brigade is Routed, Approximately 4:00 p.m.

4. At Ussher's farmstead (C) Captain Ropes' Twenty-First Regiment (4) dispatch reports of the possible threat of attack to Major General Brown at the encampment.

A Chippawa fortifications and main British lines
B Chippawa Village
C Ussher's Farmstead, location of U.S. advance post guarding the Street's Creek Bridge

1. Porter's troops (1–1a) pursue the retreating British detachments, only to break out of the forest to find themselves facing a British line (1b–1c), which opens fire with volleys.
2. After a number of volleys, the entire British Light force advances (2, 2a), routing the disrupted American force (2b, 2c).
3. On the British right flank, Norton's warriors (3) slowly advance; on the left, Major General Riall's main column revises its disposition into a staggered three-column formation. Left column: 19th Light Dragoons (3a), 100th Regiment (3b), Armstrong's artillery battery (3c), and Sheppard's artillery battery (3d). Centre column: 1st (Royal Scots) Regiment (3e). Right/reserve column: 8th (King's) Regiment (3f).

the British left flank was the artillery of Lieutenant Armstrong with two huge 24-pounder guns (usually reserved for garrison or static earthwork positions) and a five-and-a-half-inch howitzer. Next came the 100th Regiment, which would form the left flank of the infantry line, but due to some unspecified error of command, or perhaps due to the lack of room to deploy from right to left in proper company sequence, the 100th found itself deploying in a "clubbed" company formation. As such, the normal alignment placing the senior "Grenadier" company on the right of its regimental line was reversed to the far left, causing a small but critical temporary disruption in the smooth establishment of the British battle line. Further to the right, the 1st (Royal Scots) had more ground to manoeuvre and consequently deployed in its proper company order. Ideally the 8th (King's) Regiment would then have swung into line, solidifying the right flank, but unfortunately there was not enough clear ground to allow this manoeuvre and the regiment was forced to deploy slightly to the right rear of the Royal Scots. Within the resulting gap on the right of the Royals, Lieutenant Sheppard of the Royal Artillery instead

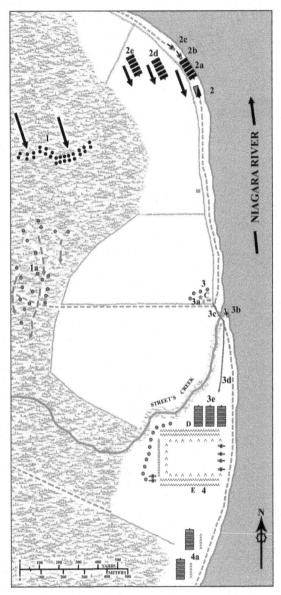

Prelude to a Battle, 4:00 –4:15 p.m.

C   Ussher's farmstead, location of U.S. advance post guarding the Street's Creek Bridge

D   Brigadier General Scott's (First Brigade) encampment

E   Brigadier General Ripley's (Second Brigade) encampment

1.   The British light troops, Canadian militias, and British Native allies (1) press forward through the forest in pursuit of the routed American Third Brigade troops and American Native allies (1a).

2.   Major General Riall's main series of columns, composed of the 19th Light Dragoons (2), the 100th Regiment (2a), Armstrong's artillery battery (2b), and Sheppard's artillery battery (2c). The 1st (Royal Scots) Regiment (2d) and the 8th (King's) Regiment (2e) approach the open fields fronting the American position.

3.   At the Ussher's farmstead (C), the American advance position (Captain Ropes' company, Twenty-First Regiment) (3) is joined by Major General Brown and his senior staff (3a). Hearing the sounds of volley fire from the forest and seeing the approaching dust cloud on the riverbank road, Brown decides to bring his army to a higher level of readiness for action, starting with the nearby Towson's artillery (3b). Major General Brown also sends his adjutant, Colonel Gardner (3c) riding back (3d) toward Brigadier General Scott's encampment (D) to bring up the First Brigade and then alert Brigadier General Ripley's Second Brigade (E). Upon arriving at Scott's encampment, Gardner finds the First Brigade already mustered, but not for action — for a drill parade! (3e)

4.   At Brigadier General Ripley's encampment (E), the general is still unaware of the heightened alert and his Brigade remains in camp (4). To the south, the remaining uncommitted elements of Brigadier General Porter's Brigade (4a) begin the establishment of their own encampment

125

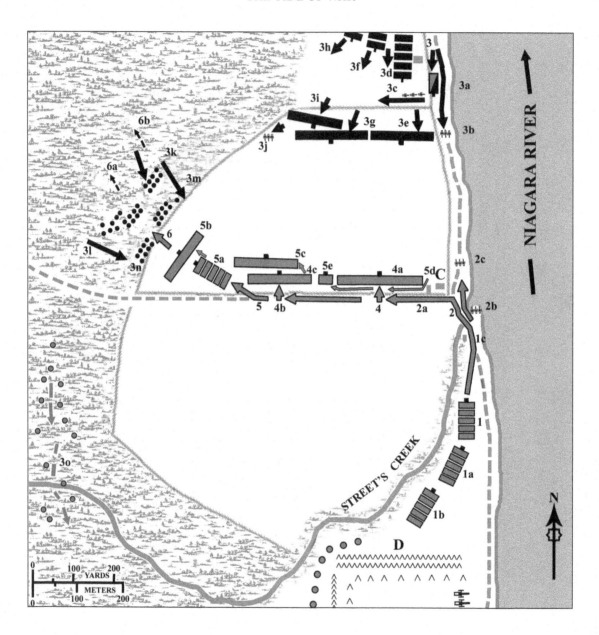

Initial Deployment and Engagement, 4:15–4:30

C   Ussher's farmstead, location of U.S. advance post guarding the Street's Creek Bridge

D   Brigadier General Scott's (First Brigade) encampment

1. Brigadier General Scott marches his First Brigade: Ninth/Twenty-Second Regiment (1), Eleventh Regiment (1a), and Twenty-Fifth Regiment (1b), along the wooded bank of Street's Creek and is therefore unable to see the approaching British force. At the Street's Creek Bridge (1c) Scott's Brigade comes under fire from Lieutenant Armstrong's battery (two 24-pounders, one 5½-inch mortar) (3b) located on the riverbank road. This fire is answered by Towson's artillery battery (two 6-pounders, one 5½-inch mortar) (2b).

2. Crossing the Street's Creek Bridge (2) Scott's Brigade turns left (2a) into the lane running behind the Ussher's farmstead (C), while Towson's artillery battery relocates to a position on the riverbank road and slightly forward of the Ussher's farm (2b, 2c). From here it recommences counter-battery fire on the British artillery.

3. Simultaneous to 1 and 2, the British deploy into line-of-battle. On the riverbank road, the 19th Light Dragoons (3) halt. The artillery advances (3a), with Armstrong's battery unlimbering on the riverbank road (3b), while Sheppard's battery moves toward the British right flank (3c). The 100th Regiment (3d) advances and forms the left of the infantry line (3e). The 1st (Royal Scots) Regiment (3f) deploys in the centre (3g). The 8th (King's) Regiment (3h) also advances, but due to the lack of open ground on the right flank is forced to deploy to the rear (3i). Sheppard's artillery battery (three 6-pounders) (3j) deploys and opens fire as

the right flank of the main British line. Within the forest, the British light troops (3k, 3l) advance to the edge of the wood line (3m, 3n) threatening the American left flank, but cease pursuing Brigadier General Porter's troops (3o).

4. The Ninth/Twenty-Second Regiment (4) wheels right, breaches the fence to enter the field, and deploys into line (4a). Similarly, the Eleventh Regiment (4b) deploys into line (4c).

5. Seeing the British light threat (3m, 3n), Scott orders the Twenty-Fifth Regiment (5) to advance and disperse the enemy. During its advance (5a), the Twenty-Fifth comes under heavy fire from the British troops in the forest, as well as Sheppard's artillery (3j), but still forms line (5b) and opens fire. Scott also moves the Eleventh Regiment forward and to the left (5c) to outflank the British line. The resulting gap is filled by relocating Ropes' company from Ussher's farmstead (C) to fill the gap (5d, 5e).

6. The Twenty-Fifth line (6) advances to the wood line, delivers three volleys, and presses into the forest. In response, the British Light troops begin to retreat (6a, 6b).

placed his three 6-pounder cannons. Finally the small detachment of 19th Light Dragoons took post to the rear of Armstrong's guns, completing the initial British formation.

In opposition to this, the somewhat chagrined Winfield Scott pressed forward his First Brigade across the Street's Creek bridge while under fire. Off to his right, Captain Towson of the U.S. Artillery, having already opened fire on Armstrong's British guns, now ceased fire, limbered his guns (two 6-pounders and a five-and-a-half-inch howitzer) and also advanced across the bridge, before establishing his battery alongside the Ussher farmstead and recommencing counter-battery fire on Armstrong's position. Wheeling left from the bridge, Scott marched his column along a lane that ran west from the river road behind the Ussher Farm. He then swung the formation to the right and moved into the open field in front and began deploying his own troops in the classic line formation. Anchored on the right by Towson's guns, the American line now consisted of the combined Ninth/Twenty-Second Regiment on the right, the Eleventh Regiment in the centre, while the Twenty-Fifth Regiment continued to move to the left in column. Having seen considerable battlefield service and having practised long and hard over the previous months, the Ninth/Twenty-Second and Eleventh reacted to the current situation with calm efficiency and discipline. Watching from the other side of the field, Major General Riall realized that despite the grey coats worn by these troops (which had previously misled him into believing them to be relatively undisciplined militia troops, such as those he had routed at Buffalo only six months before) he was, in fact, facing regularly trained and fully disciplined regiments, to which he is reputed to have stated, "Why these are regulars by God!"[5]

At this point, elements of Pearson's red-coated light troops and groups of Native Warriors began to appear along the wood line, in front of the American left. In response, Scott revised his formation even as it was forming and, instead of having the Twenty-Fifth turn and form line, he directed them to move across the open ground to deal with this threat. He also moved the Eleventh further to the left, leaving a gap between it and the combined unit of the Ninth/Twenty-Second. Under normal circumstances this would create a dangerous weak spot in a battle line, but this was partially filled as the advance picket from the Twenty-First Infantry Regiment (Captain Ropes), located at Ussher's Farm, was moved across into the opening.

As the two infantry formations were still beyond effective musket range, the only firing at this point was between the artillery batteries on the flanks. Nearest the river, Towson's battery and Armstrong's guns inflicted casualties on each other in an attempt to gain mastery of that flank, each losing the use of a gun in the process. Across the field, Sheppard's guns had a clear target in the form of the Twenty-Fifth advancing across the open ground toward the woods. Opening up with roundshot at a range of around 400 yards (366 meters), his guns quickly inflicted a number of casualties as the solid spheres bowled through the densely packed column.

After seeing the artillery doing effective duty on the enemy, Major General Riall decided the time was right to close on the enemy with his line.

The formation to his front had proved it was fully capable of deploying and forming under fire and was no mere militia that would run at the first sign of fighting, but its numbers corresponded with that of his intelligence reports as roughly equal to his own. Confident in the superiority of his own troops in a toe-to-toe firefight, he ordered the 100th and 1st (Royal Scots) regiments forward, while bringing the 8th (King's) Regiment up at an angle to counter the movement of the Twenty-Fifth Regiment.

Inevitably, this forward movement masked (blocked the firing of) both of the British gun batteries, forcing Armstrong (on the left) to cease fire and limber up his guns prior to moving forward to a new position where he would have a clear line of fire. However, Sheppard's battery was unable to move up and became completely blocked on the British right, allowing the Americans a momentary respite before the lines closed to effective killing range. Viewing the advance, Winfield Scott realized that the angled advance of the 8th (King's) line was creating a gap between its left flank and the right flank of the 1st (Royal Scots) and that his own formation extended past the foreshortened main British line. He therefore ordered the Eleventh to swing its left flank forward so that it could commence firing obliquely into the exposed Royal Scots flank. Scott then rode across the entire American line to Towson's

battery and redirected its fire onto the advancing British line in a similar oblique fashion.

As the lines closed to less than one hundred yards (91 meters) apart, the first American volleys tore into the redcoat formation, bringing it to a momentary halt. True to its discipline, however, the line absorbed the punishment, closed ranks, and continued its march forward, only to receive further volleys of musketfire and point-blank cannonfire from Towson's guns. Brought to a complete halt, the British line returned the compliment of musketry on the Americans, likewise creating gaps that were quickly filled as the companies closed on their colours. Volley followed volley from both lines and the dogged determination of each force not to budge or waver only served to increase the toll of casualties, especially amongst the 100th Regiment, who were directly in front of Towson's guns and had entire segments of their line scythed away with each blast from the American battery. Nor were the 1st (Royal Scots) in a much better position on the right, as the American Eleventh Regiment used their advantageous flanking position to pour in their deadly volleys.

During this same interval, on the American left flank, Jesup's Twenty-Fifth Regiment completed its oblique movement across the field and approached the woods where the British light companies, militia, and Natives were massing. Ignoring

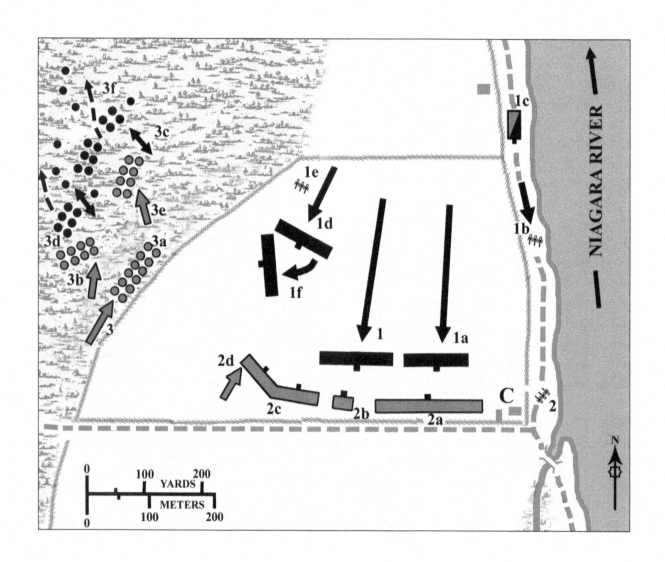

Close Quarter Slaughter, 4:30–5:15 p.m.

C. Ussher's farmstead

1. Determined to close with the enemy, Major General Riall orders the 1st (Royal Scots) Regiment (1) and 100th Regiment (1a) to advance in line directly toward the centre of the American line. In support, Armstrong's battery moves (1b) down the river-bank road, covered by the 19th Light Dragoons (1c). The 8th (King's) Regiment (1d) advances to the right, thereby "masking" (blocking the firing of) Sheppard's battery (1e) and preventing it from providing supporting fire. As it advances, the 8th (Kings) is threatened by the Twenty-Fifth troops at the wood line (3a) and forced to wheel right (1f), preventing it from completing the formation of the main British firing line.

2. Towson's artillery (2) switches its fire from Armstrong's guns (1b) and targets the approaching left flank of the 100th Regiment (1a). The Ninth/Twenty-Second Regiment (2a) and Ropes Company, Twenty-First Regiment (2b) and Eleventh Regiment (2c) also open fire as the British line comes within range. However, due to the detachment of the 8th (Kings) Regiment (1f), the British line is foreshortened. In response, the Eleventh Regiment wheels forward its left wing (2d), enfilading the British line.

3. Simultaneous to 1 and 2, the Twenty-Fifth Regiment (3) advance along the fence line (3a) threatening the flank of the 8th (King's) Regiment (1f), while Captain Ketchum's company (3b) is detached to pursue the retreating enemy, only to be counter-attacked by the regrouped British light troops (3c–3d). In response, Ketchum is forced to call for reinforcements (3e), which arrive and force the British to make a fighting retreat (3f).

the intermittent fire coming from the enemy to his front and the occasional shot from Sheppard's guns, Jesup now formed his regiment into line and opened fire. After a succession of volleys he then advanced in line, halting immediately outside of the wood line, fired three volleys into the disorganized British units and charged with the bayonet. Inevitably the Natives and militia melted back into the woods before this disciplined onslaught. Beside them, the regulars, heavily outnumbered and not properly reformed, were also forced to give ground, leaving the Americans in an advantageous position to move along the wood line and outflank the approaching 8th (King's) Regiment. Detaching Captain Ketchum's company to pursue the retreating British light troops, Jesup reformed his remaining force along the fence bordering the forest and opened fire into the flank of the 8th (King's), which forced it to halt its advance and change its front to meet this new threat, thus increasing the gap between it and the remainder of the line. Additional volleys and a further advance along the flank by Jesup's troops again compelled the 8th (King's) to change position to face the American fire. Fortunately for the 8th (King's), the British light troops regrouped in the woods and took on Ketchum's company, compelling him to call for reinforcements from Jesup, effectively ending his movement around the British flank. Nevertheless, Jesup's actions effectively prevented the 8th (King's) from closing on the fore-shortened British line, which would otherwise have terminated the deadly flanking fire of the Eleventh Regiment on the 1st (Royal Scots).

As a result, the main battle stalled and became a brutal matter of face-to-face pounding and attrition, as neither side could advance and neither was willing to retire. In this kind of competition, the advantage lay with the Americans, as Major General Riall had no reinforcements whatsoever, while Major General Brown now had the entire Second Brigade on the move toward Street's Creek. However, instead of sending it along the direct and open road to the battlefield, which would have quickly brought this force into action at the crisis of the battle, Brown ordered Ripley to move off into the dense forest and push forward in a wide sweep to the west. By this he hoped to see Ripley's troops surprise the British right flank or even succeed in getting behind, thus cutting the enemy off from retreating. He similarly directed Brigadier General Porter, who had succeeded in reforming part of his Third Brigade, including those that had not previously joined his initial attack, to make a parallel advance. However, both of these formations soon found themselves bogged down in the dense forest and unable to press forward with any speed, significantly delaying their commitment to the battle that was raging ahead.

The deciding factor in the battle came shortly afterward as fresh batteries of artillery (Richie's company with two 6-pounders and a five-and-a-half-inch howitzer and Biddle's company with a 12-pounder, under Lieutenant Hall) came up the riverbank road and moved into a firing position between the Eleventh and Ninth/Twenty-Second regiments. From this vantage point, the additional American guns opened up at point-blank range, tearing unfillable gaps in the already-depleted ranks of the British line. Under the cumulative slaughter of this remorseless and increasing assault, the British line began to recoil, beginning with the flanks, which had suffered most throughout the entire conflict. Seeing his force involuntarily beginning to lose ground, and perhaps noting an increasing number of American troops infiltrating along the western wood line, Major General Riall ordered a general withdrawal. Defeated, but not beaten, the 100th and 1st (Royal Scots) regiments disengaged and retired their reduced line out of musket range before forming a relatively orderly column and marching from the field, covered by the relatively intact formations of the 8th (King's) and Light Dragoons.

Despite being elated by their success, the men of the First American Brigade had also suffered significant casualties and were in a partial state of disorder. They therefore did not immediately advance on the retreating British, but paused to regroup and reform their lines before marching forward, stepping over the distinct lines of British dead and wounded that marked the points at which the earlier British advance had been brought to a halt. Any attempt to turn the British retreat into a rout was foiled, however, by the strong rearguard of the 8th (King's) Regiment and the 19th Light Dragoons, who denied the Americans the trophy of a disabled cannon in Armstrong's battery by using their horses as draft animals to drag it from the field.

Reaching the Chippawa bridge, the British crossed unmolested and formed up behind their entrenchments, while the rearguard began demolishing the roadbed as the first American units appeared on the riverbank road. At the same time, groups of British Natives and militia, which had been fighting in the dense woods throughout the afternoon, began to emerge from the treeline and were forced to run for the bridge under fire from the American troops to save themselves from being cut off. Hoping to stall the American advance and give time for the last groups of Natives to cross, not to mention exact reprisals for their defeat, the British artillery batteries, located in the fieldworks on the north side of the Chippawa River, opened up on the Americans. This forced Winfield Scott's column to halt their approach to the bridge and seek cover by lying down in their ranks to await reinforcements.

Shortly thereafter, Brigadier General Porter arrived with his reformed units and joined Winfield Scott's brigade in lying prone to avoid taking unnecessary casualties. From this vantage point they saw the last of the bridge roadbed removed and those of Norton's Natives still on the south bank working their way across the upright pilings of the bridge.

About a half-hour later, Major General Brown arrived, accompanying Brigadier General Ripley's brigade, and the combined group of commanders discussed the options for the army. Despite the fact that there was only an hour or two of daylight left, the American victory had elated the Americans to the point that everyone's first judgement was to continue the attack and try to force a crossing of the Chippawa, disperse the enemy while he was still reeling from his bloody defeat, and end the campaign then and there. On the other hand, it soon became obvious that continuing the attack would be a problem, as night was approaching, giving the British the advantage. In addition, their earlier victory had only been gained at a substantial cost in killed and wounded within the First Brigade, the numbers of which were not yet assessed. Finally, the Chippawa bridge had been successfully dismantled by the British and any attempt to reach it and undertake repairs would expose the working parties to the full might of both the entrenched British gun batteries and the musket fire of every surviving enemy infantryman.

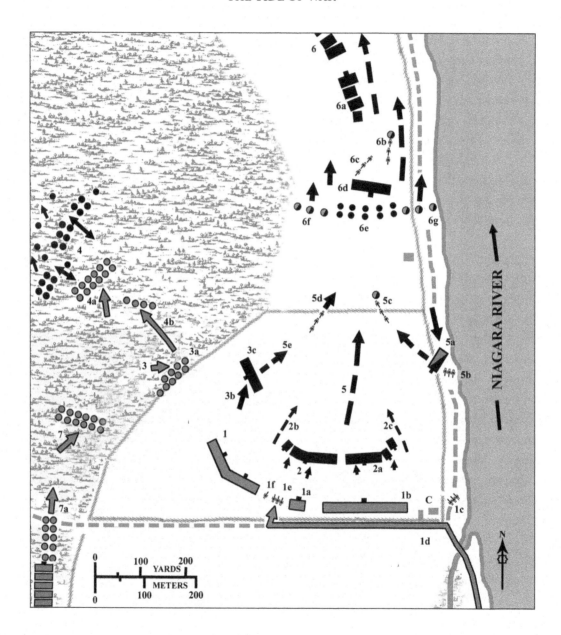

The British Position Crumbles and Disengagement

C.   Ussher's farmstead

1.   The American line: Eleventh Regiment (1), Ropes' Company, Twenty- First Regiment (1a), Ninth/ Twenty-Second Regiment (1b), Towson's artillery battery (1c) is supplemented by the arrival (1d) of artillery reinforcements, Captain Richie's battery (two 6-pounders, one 5½-inch howitzer) (1e) and a detached gun from Captain Biddle's command under Lieutenant Hall (one 12-pounder) (1f).

2.   Suffering increasing casualties the entire British line begins to recoil (2, 2a). This is escalated by the crumbling and partial retreat of the companies on both flanks (2b, 2c).

3.   At the wood line, the remaining portion of the Twenty-Fifth Regiment (3) continue their push along the fence line (3a) in an attempt to out- flank the 8th (King's) Regiment (3b), forcing it to redeploy (3c), preventing it from supporting the main British line.

4.   Deeper in the forest, the British light troops (4) continue their fighting retreat against the detached units of the Twenty-Fifth Regiment (4a), who call for additional reinforcements (4b), thus diminishing the threat on the British flank.

5.   Recognizing his gamble has failed, Major General Riall orders a general disengagement and with- drawal. The main British line retreats (5) down the centre of the field. On the riverbank road, the 19th Light Dragoons (5a) cover the retreat of Armstrong's artillery (5b) but are forced to use some of their horses to pull off the guns (5c). Sheppard's battery also retires (5d), covered by the 8th (King's) Regiment (5e).

6.   As the American line does not immediately press forward in an attack, the British are able to reform and conduct a relatively orderly retreat: 100th Regiment (6), 1st (Royal Scots) Regiment (6a), Armstrong's battery (6b), Sheppard's battery (6c). The rearguard is composed of the 8th (King's) Regiment in line (6d), fronted by a screen of troops in extended skirmish order (6e). On the flanks, detachments of the 19th Light Dragoons (6f, 6g) also provide rearguard cover.

7.   As the main American line prepares to advance, the leading elements of Brigadier General Porter's reformed Third Division (7) and Brigadier Ripley's Second Division (7a) begin to appear from the wood line on the south west of the field, too late to join the action.

After detailing his aides to make a thorough reconnaissance and report, Major General Brown ordered his army back to its encampment to prepare for further operations the following day.

For his part, Major General Riall was now placed in the difficult position of reporting his defeat to his superior, Lieutenant General Drummond, and then up the chain of command to Prevost and Whitehall. His subsequent explanation referred to his attack as "not attended with the success that I had hoped for...."[6] While crediting the Americans for their improved quality of battlefield effort, Riall clearly attributed his reversal to an overwhelming number of American troops in their line-of-battle (estimating the American force at over 6,000 versus his own 1,800).

Looking west across the preserved Chippawa battlefield in 2013.

By making this excuse, however, he conveniently chose to ignore the inherent contradiction of this claim in comparison to his original reasoning for initiating an attack on the Americans, instead of remaining securely on the defensive behind his lines at Chippawa. Not to mention the extended period of time his troops stood face-to-face with this enemy, exchanging volleys at point-blank range. In other words, if the Americans really had openly fielded that many troops in the first place, neither Riall, nor any other competent commander would have been so foolish as to attack

them on their own ground. Likewise, had these "superior numbers"[7] appeared during the initial or even central course of the engagement, he would have gone on the defensive or broken off much earlier; recognizing the fact that he had absolutely no reserve to counterbalance the American advantage of numbers.

Fortunately for Riall, Lieutenant General Drummond recognized the calamitous effect this defeat of British regulars by an equivalent number of American troops could have on morale and the further prosecution of the war effort. He therefore chose to publicly support Riall's line of reasoning of bravely fighting against overwhelming American numbers, as did Prevost. Privately, however, both senior commanders realized that this European-style collision of lines had produced the unexpected result of proving that the Americans were now fully capable of fielding an army that was able to contend with whatever the British had to offer — and the humiliating defeats and debacles of the American army over the previous two years were now things of the past.

The monument to the Battle of Chippawa, located on the otherwise almost pristine and intact open field that was the Chippawa battlefield, the only such location within the entire catalogue of 1812 related sites on the Niagara frontier.

**OFFICIAL CASUALTY RETURNS,
BATTLE OF CHIPPAWA, JULY 5, 1814[8]**

American

First Brigade

Killed	2 musicians, 39 other ranks
Wounded	9 officers, 1 musician, 212 other ranks

Second Brigade

Killed	3 other ranks
Wounded	3 other ranks
Missing / Prisoners	2 other ranks

Third Brigade

Killed	3 other ranks
Wounded	2 other ranks
Missing / Prisoners	1 officer, 4 other ranks

American Native Allies

Killed	9–15 Warriors
Wounded	4 Warriors
Missing / Prisoners	10 Warriors
Artillery	
Killed	4 gunners
Wounded	16 gunners

British

British Regulars

Killed	3 officers, 132 other ranks
Wounded	21 officers, 268 other ranks
Missing/Prisoners	1 officer, 30 other ranks

Canadian Militia

Killed	3 officers, 9 other ranks
Wounded	4 officers, 12 other ranks
Missing/Prisoners	15 other ranks

Cavalry

Wounded	6 other ranks

Artillery

Killed	1 other ranks
Wounded	1 officer, 4 other ranks

British Native allies

Killed	87 Warriors*
Wounded	Number unknown
Missing / Prisoners	5 Warriors*

(*N.B. Due to the departure of the British Native allies immediately following the battle, this figure is derived from an American report and the killed total may well include Natives who fought for the Americans and who are mistakenly claimed as British losses, having lost their identifying head cloths during the fight. The same American report also claims to have inflicted casualties of a total of 10 officers and 298 other ranks upon the British.)

In response, both Riall and Drummond resolved to take the threat of the American army on the Niagara far more seriously. Drummond also recognized that he might need to take a more immediate and direct command of his troops if the military situation continued to deteriorate. For Riall, although he had regained his lines without contest and was temporarily secure, the shock of seeing his force beaten by an army that he had previously held in contempt undermined his resolve and caused him to react with excessive caution during the following weeks as the campaign developed. For both armies, the close-quarters, European style of battle had caused the expected heavy casualties.[8] What was different, however, was that neither side could quickly obtain additional troops to replace their losses. Furthermore, the relatively small sizes of the contending forces meant that the death of dozens of men in a battle on the Niagara frontier carried the same strategic importance as that of hundreds on the battlefields of Spain, or thousands in Russia.

CHAPTER 10

The High Tide

Following their defeat at Chippawa, many British officers believed that Major General Riall had erred in going on the offensive before his available reinforcements had all arrived. Having suffered so severely, virtually all of the surviving Natives not loyal to Norton quit the Chippawa position, as did many of the militia, thus depriving Riall of most of his light troops and weakening his position. Desperate to replace these losses, orders were immediately dispatched for all remaining regular and militia forces to join the army on the Niagara and attempt to hold back the Americans, despite having to leave their former garrison positions entirely undefended.

For his part, although victorious, Major General Brown recognized that this success had only been achieved at the cost of a substantial number of casualties from the force that had trained for so long that spring. Nor were there any equivalent troops that could take their place. In addition, having successfully regained the far bank of the Chippawa, the British now blocked the only road available to reach the mouth of the Niagara and the expected rendezvous with Chauncey's fleet on July 10. As his troops evacuated the wounded and prisoners across the Niagara River and buried the dead of both sides in long common graves upon the field of battle, Major General Brown decided to explore the possibility of outflanking the British defences by crossing the Chippawa River further upstream. To this end, scouts brought back reports that the narrow lane that ran behind the Ussher farmstead and into the forest could be widened to allow formations of troops to reach a point where a pontoon

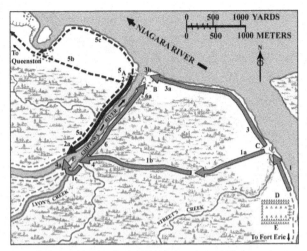

The American Flanking Movement and Engagement at Weishoun's Point, July 8, 1814.

A   Chippawa fortifications and main British lines
B   Chippawa Village
C   Ussher's farmstead
D   Brigadier General Scott's (First Brigade) encampment
E   Brigadier General Ripley's (Second Brigade) encampment

1. Following two days of intensive work to expand the narrow forest trail that connects the Ussher farmstead (C) with Weishoun's Point (F), the American army moves out from its encampment (D, E) on July 8th (1). At the Ussher farmstead, Brigadier General Ripley's (Second Brigade) and Brigadier General Porter's (Third Brigade) move west (1a) and enter the forest. Almost immediately, the brigades find the trackway is incapable of allowing the passage of the accompanying wagons and artillery. It therefore becomes necessary to undertake additional work to clear and widen the roadway, which slows the advance (1b) and creates significant noise, effectively ruining any chance of surprise. Reaching the bank of Lyon's Creek at Weishoun's Point (F), they find British units already in situ on the other side of the Chippawa (Welland) River (2a).

2. Receiving reports at the Chippawa position (A) of activity on the American side of the Chippawa River behind Weihoun's Point (F), Major General Riall sends detachments of infantry and artillery under Lieutenant Colonel Pearson to occupy the position opposite the point (2, 2a).

3. Brigadier General Scott's (First Brigade) (3) marches along the riverbank road (3a) with orders to make a strong diversionary show of force at the Chippawa Village (B) to persuade the British that an attempt would be made to cross there (3b).

4. Faced with the loss of surprise and British forces in opposition, Brigadier General Ripley halts the advance (4) and sends word to Major General Brown. Brown arrives and takes command. He then orders the attack recommenced and begins construction of a pontoon bridge while under fire (4a).

5. Faced with Scott's apparent plan to cross at the bridge (3b), Major General Riall (5) is unable to send reinforcements to Pearson (2a). Subsequently receiving erroneous reports that the Americans had succeeded in crossing at Weishoun's Point, Riall believes his position has been turned. He therefore orders a general evacuation from the Chippawa line (A) (5a, 5b, 5c).

6. Receiving reports from Scott (3b) that the British are evacuating their defences at Chippawa (A), Brown discontinues his bridge building and marches the Second and Third brigades (6) along the Chippawa riverbank toward the bridge (6a) to unite his force before making his crossing at the now burned-out village of Chippawa (B).

Looking west along the Chippawa (Welland) River from Chippawa toward Weishoun's Point, where the Americans attempted their outflanking manoeuvre on July 8, 1814 (crossing from left to right).

depleted First Brigade to keep the attention of the British focused on the prospect of a direct assault. He then sent Brigadier General Ripley's (Second) and Brigadier General Porter's (Third) brigades to construct the necessary bridge across to the north bank and attack the British from the rear. Contrary to Brown's understanding, however, the route to Lyon's Creek was still far from being properly cleared and the advancing columns were delayed in their march as more engineering work was required to create a passable road for the artillery and wagons carrying the timber and boats. Furthermore, once at the intended crossing point, the Americans found that their roadwork had alerted the British pickets and that Major General Riall had dispatched a force of regulars (Colonel Pearson with the flank companies of the 1st [Royal Scots], and artillerymen with three 6-pounder guns) to contest the crossing.

Unwilling to see his troops suffer the heavy casualties that would inevitably result if he attempted to build a bridge while under fire, Ripley held his position while sending a report back to Brown. In response, an angry Major General Brown came forward and personally took over command from Ripley, ordering the troops forward while using his superior firepower in artillery to bombard the far shore. Despite taking casualties among the work parties, the bridge was pushed to the midpoint

bridge could be constructed at Weishoun's Point, located at the junction of Lyon's Creek and the Chippawa River. After making a personal inspection the following morning, Brown ordered the use of supply boats stationed at the American camp to be hauled overland for use as floatation supports, while timber stripped from the Ussher and Street farmsteads would be used as construction materials for the bridge's roadbed. He also detached teams of men to widen the narrow trail to the projected crossing point. By that evening, he was informed that the passage was suitable for use.

On the morning of July 8, Major General Brown ordered Brigadier General Winfield Scott's

A modern (2013) view of the location where Ripley's force attempted to construct a pontoon bridge to cross the Chippawa (Welland) River.

1. Lyon's Creek
2. Weishoun's Point
3. Chippawa (Welland) River
4. The north bank, where the British established their positions

5. To the Chippawa bridge and the Niagara River
6. The rotted wooden pilings of a bridge similar in construction to that built across the Chippawa at the time of the war

F.C. Christian, artist (after G. Heriot), 1807. The view of the Great Falls of Niagara from upriver at the hamlet of Bridgewater.

A.M. Hoffy, artist (after J. Vanderlyn), c.1840. The Great Falls of Niagara, as seen from below Table Rock in 1801.

of the river when a report arrived that the British appeared to be abandoning their defences at Chippawa and marching north. This report being confirmed, the construction of the pontoon bridge was abandoned and the column retraced its steps to rendezvous with Scott's forces at the mouth of the Chippawa.

For his part, Major General Riall had been confident of his ability to defend the main crossing point on the Chippawa but, recognizing that his right flank was partially exposed, he took the precaution of establishing pickets out in the bush and sending all non-essential supplies back to Queenston Heights. As he feared, the Americans did make a move to his right on July 8th and he

Right: The spectacular panoramic view of the lower reaches of the Niagara River and Lake Ontario as seen from the top of the Niagara escarpment above Queenston.

1. Queenston
2. Vrooman's Point
3. Lewiston NY
4. Fort George/Newark (Niagara-on-the-Lake)
5. Fort Niagara
6. The north shore of Lake Ontario/York (Toronto)

(Below) The same perspective in 2013.

dispatched Pearson's holding force, which later requested reinforcements as the Americans were making a determined effort to cross the Chippawa. Unable to send the requested support, due to the threat of Scott's troops at his front, Riall later received an erroneous report of a successful American crossing. In response, he decided that the threat of encirclement rendered the Chippawa line redundant and ordered a retreat toward Queenston. Withdrawing his force under the cover of a severe rainstorm, Riall met up with the Volunteer Battalion of Incorporated Militia, marching toward the Chippawa River. This regiment had been rapidly pushed over from York in response to Riall's call for reinforcements and had just made a forced march to join the line, only to be now told to join the retreat as its rearguard. Continuing north, Riall moved his troops on with some rapidity, concerned that the Americans might outflank him or cut him off by sending a second force across at Lewiston/Queenston. After a hurried march, he reached Fort George late that night and set about developing plans for a new line of defence.

Back at the Chippawa River, Major General Brown ferried the First and Second brigades over the river during the night of July 8th/9th, while ordering Brigadier General Porter's Third Brigade to repair the bridge and then bring forward the main baggage train. Pressing forward, Brown's troops met with only token resistance and reached the heights at Queenston, from which the general could see across the plain to Lake Ontario and his expected place of rendezvous with Commodore Chauncey. Here the American army encamped and was later joined by Porter's brigade, as well as additional reinforcements that were badly needed to bring the army back up to strength. The only thing missing was Chauncey and his fleet. By the fourth day of waiting and watching, however, Brown's patience had reached its limit and he penned a strongly worded letter off to the Commodore:

My Dear Sir … I arrived at this place on the 10th, as I assured you that with the blessing of God I would…. Meet me on the lakeshore north of Fort George with your fleet and we will be able to … break the power of the enemy in Upper Canada and that in the course of a short time. At all events, let me hear from you. I have looked for your fleet with the greatest anxiety since the 10th…. We can threaten Forts George and Niagara, carry Burlington Heights and York and proceed direct to Kingston and carry that place. For Gods sake let me see you…. If you conclude to meet me … and that immediately, have the goodness to bring the guns and troops that I have ordered from the harbor: at all events have the politeness to let me know what aid I am to expect from the fleet of Lake Ontario....[1]

> — Major General Brown to
> Commodore Chauncey, July 13, 1814

What he did not know was that he was about to get a nasty surprise, for the American military "tide" had now reached its peak and was about to turn. This story will be continued in the next part of this series, *A Crucible of Fire*.

NOTES

A star indicates the note refers to a sidebar.

ABBREVIATIONS:

LAC: Library and Archives of Canada.

AOO: Archives of Ontario.

CRDH: Ernest Cruikshank, *The Documentary History of the Campaigns upon the Niagara Frontier 1812–1814*, 9 Volumes (Welland, ON: Tribune Press, 1896–1908).

CGMC: Buffalo and Erie County Historical Society Archives, B00-11, A. Conger Goodyear War of 1812 Manuscripts, 1779–1862.

SBD1812:   William C.H. Wood, *Select British Documents of the War of 1812* (Toronto: Champlain Society of Canada, 1920).

CHAPTER 1: INTRODUCTION

1. Government of the United States, *Causes of the Failure of the Army on the Northern Frontier*, Report to the House of Representatives, February 2, 1814, 13th Congress, 2nd Session, Military Affairs, Vol. 1.

CHAPTER 2: DEALING A NEW HAND AND UPPING THE ANTE

1. CRDH, Vol. 9, 138.
2. LAC, RG8-I: British Military and Naval Records, 1757–1903, Vol. 1222, 14.
3. CRDH Vol. 9, 208–09.
4. CRDH Vol. 9, 235.
5. CRDH Vol. 9, 247.
*6. R. Malcomson, *Warships of the Great Lakes, 1754–1834* (London: Chatham Publishing, 2001), 100–18.
7. War Office to Wilkinson, April 24, 1814, LAC, MG11. CO42, Vol. 160, 377.
8. CGMC, Vol. 9, Miscellaneous Letters.

CHAPTER 3: THE WINTER OF DISCONTENT IN THE WEST

1. CRDH, Vol. 9, 208.
2. CRDH, Vol. 9, 204.
3. CRDH, Vol. 9, 204–05.
*4. CRDH, Vol. 9, 219.
5. CRDH, Vol. 9, 224.
*6. G. Stott, *Greater Evils, The War of 1812 in South Western Ontario* (G. Private Publication, 2001), 110–11.
7. CRDH, Vol. 9, 230.
8. *Ibid.*
9. *Ibid.*
10. CRDH, Vol. 9, 223–26.
11. CRDH, Vol. 9, 231.
12. *Ibid.*
13. *Ibid.*
14. *Ibid.*
15. *Ibid.*
*16. CRDH, Vol. 9, 205.
17. CRDH, Vol. 9, 218.
*18. CRDH, Vol. 9, 219.
19. CRDH, Vol. 9, 225.

CHAPTER 4: MARCHING IN A NEW DIRECTION — OR TWO

1. C. Chapin, *Chapin's Review of Armstrong's Notices of the War of 1812* (Black Rock, NY: Private Publication, Black Rock, 1836), 213.
2. C. Elliott, *Winfield Scott, the Soldier and the Man* (Toronto: The Macmillan Company of Canada Ltd. 1937), 148.
3. H. Adams, *History of the United States of America During the Administrations of Madison* (New York: Library of America, 1986, reprint of original 1891 volumes), Vol. 2, 28.

CHAPTER 5: THE ATTACK THAT NEVER WAS

1. SBD1812, Vol. 3, Part 1, 40–42.
2. SBD1812, Vol. 3, Part 1, 44–45.
3. SBD1812, Vol. 3, Part 1, 47–48.
4. SBD1812, Vol. 3, Part 1, 49–51.
*5. CRDH, Vol. 9, 322–23, 328–29.

CHAPTER 6: THE RAID ON OSWEGO

*1. CRDH, Vol. 9, 322–23, 328–29.
2. CRDH Vol. 9, 350–51.
3. SBD1812, Vol. 3, Part 1, 78–80.

CHAPTER 7: BUILDING A NEW ARMY

1. General Order, June 13, 1814. A. Bowler (ed.), *War Along the Niagara, Essays on the War of 1812 and its Legacy* (Youngstown, NY: Old Fort Niagara Association, 1991), 46.
2. *Ibid.* General Scott to General Winder, May 6, 1814, 43.
3. CRDH, Vol. 2, 372–73.
4. Previously undocumented photocopy of an original handwritten manuscript in the author's possession, 5th page. Possibly originally sourced at the William L. Clements Library, University of Michigan.
*5. Wright, *The Burning of Dover*, 25.
6. SBD1812, Vol. 3, Part 1, 88–89.
7. CRDH, Vol. 1, 17.
8. *Ibid.*

CHAPTER 8: THE INVASION OF JULY 1814

*1. CRDH Vol. 2, 408.
2. Niagara Historical Society Papers No. 30.
3. *Ibid.*
4. *Ibid.*
5. CRDH, Vol. 2, 404.

6. Winfield Scott, *Memoirs of Lieutenant General Scott* (New York: Sheldon & Co., 1864). State Historical Monographs, Historical Literature Collection, Anonymous collection, *circa* 1850.
*7. CRDH Vol. 1, 28–30.
*8. CGMC, Vol. 14; Thomas S. Jesup, *Jesup's Memoirs of the Campaign of 1814*, 3.
*9. LAC, RG8-I: British Military and Naval Records, 1757–1903, Vol. 1, 77–79.

CHAPTER 9: THE BATTLE OF CHIPPAWA

*1. SBD1812, Vol. 3 Part 1, 115–20.
*2. SBD1812, Vol. 3 Part 1, 111.
3. CGMG, Vol. 13, Peter B. Porter Letters.
4. CGMC, Vol. 3, Brown, J., "Memoranda of Occurrences and Some Important Facts Attending the Campaign on the Niagara," 6.
5. Scott, *Memoirs of Lieutenant General Scott*; State Historical Monographs, Historical Literature Collection, Anonymous collection, *circa* 1850, 129.
6. SBD1812, Vol. 3, Part 1, 115–16; and CRDH Vol. 1, 32.
7. *Ibid.*
*8. LAC, RG8-I: British Military and Naval Records, 1757–1903, Vol. 1219, 248 SDB1812, Vol. 3 Part 1, 110–11; CRDH Vol. 1, 42–43.

CHAPTER 10: THE HIGH TIDE

1. CRDH, Vol. 1, 64.

SELECTED BIBLIOGRAPHY

PRIMARY SOURCES

Archival
1. Library and Archives of Canada
    Manuscript Groups (MG)
        MG10A: U.S. Department of State, War of 1812 Records
        MG11 (CO42): British Colonial Office, Original Correspondence, Canada
        MG11 (CO47): Upper Canada Records, 1764–1836, Miscellaneous
        MG13 (WO62): Commissariat Dept, Miscellaneous Records 1809–14
        MG19/A39: Duncan Clark Papers
        MG24/A9: Sir George Prevost Papers
    Research Groups (RG)
        RG5-A1: Civil Secretary's Office, Upper Canada Sundries, 1791–1867
        RG8-I: British Military and Naval Records, 1757–1903
        RG9-I: Pre-Confederation Records, Military
        RG10: Indian Department Records
        RG19/E5A: Department of Finance, War of 1812, Losses Board

2. Archives Ontario
        MS35/1: Strachan Papers
        MS74/R5: Merritt Papers
        MS501: Thorburn Papers
        MS58: Band Papers
        MS500: Street Papers
        MS519: Joel Stone Papers
        MS 520: Solomon Jones Papers
        MS502/B Series: Nelles Papers
        MU2099: A.A. Rapelje Papers
        MU527: Duncan Clark Papers
        MU2034: Events in the Military History of the Saint Lawrence River Valley 1779–1814
        MS74.R5: Henry Ruttan Papers
        Microfilm B91/Reel 1: Table of Statutes, Upper Canada Legislature 1792–1840

3. Metro Toronto Reference Library
        Hagerman, C.: Journal of Christopher Hagerman
        MacDonell, G.: MacDonell Papers
        Prevost Papers, 7 Vols., S108, Cub 7

4. Detroit Public Library Archives
    Kirby, J.: James Kirby Papers

5. Buffalo and Erie County Historical Society Archives, A. Conger Goodyear War of 1812 Manuscripts, 1779–1862, Mss. BOO-11, 16 Volumes

Early Secondary Publications

Armstrong, J. *Notices of the War of 1812*. New York: Wiley & Putnam, 1840.

Boyd, J.P. *Documents and Facts Relative to Military Events during the Late War*. Private publication, 1816.

Brackenridge, Henry. M. *History of the Late War Between the United States and Great Britain*. Cushing & Jewett, 1817.

Brannan, J. *Official Letters of the Military and Naval Officers of the United States, during the War with Great Britain in the years 1812, 13, 14, & 15*. Washington City: Way & Gideon, 1823.

Chapin, C. *Chapin's Review of Armstrong's Notices of the War of 1812*. Black Rock, NY: Private publication, 1836.

Davis, Paris M. *An Authentick History of the Late War Between the United States and Great Britain*. Ithica, NY: Mack & Andrus, 1829.

_____. *The Four Principal Battles of the Late War Between the United States and Great Britain*. Harrisburg, NY: Jacob Baab, 1832.

Dawson, M. *A Historical Narrative of the True Civil and Military Services of Major-General William H. Harrison*. Cincinnati: M. Dawson, Cincinnati Advertiser Office, 1824.

Dearborn, H.A.S. *Defence of Gen. Henry Dearborn Against the Attack of Gen. William Hull*. Boston: E.W. Davies, 1824.

Gilleland, J.C. *History of the Late War Between the United States and Great Britain*. Baltimore, MD: Schaeffer & Maund, 1817.

Hitsman, J.M. *History of the American War of Eighteen Hundred and Twelve*. Philadelphia: W. McCarty, 1816.

James, W. *A Full and Correct Account of the Military Occurrences of the Late War Between Great Britain and the United States of America*. London: William James, 1818.

McCarty, W. *History of the American War of 1812*. Philadelphia: William McCarty & Davis, 1817.

Merritt, William Hamilton. *Journal of Events: Principally on the Detroit & Niagara Frontiers during the War of 1812*. St. Catharines, CW: Canada West Historical Society, 1863.

Morgan, J.C. *The Emigrant's Guide, With Recollections of Upper and Lower Canada during the Late War Between the United States of America and Great Britain*. London: Longman, Hurst, Rees, Orme & Brown, 1824.

O'Connor, T. *An Impartial and Correct History of the War Between the United States of America and Great Britain*. Belfast: Joseph Smyth, 1816. Reprint of the John Low edition, New York, 1815.

Official Correspondence with the Department of War relative to the Military Operations of the American Army under the Command of Major General Izard of the Northern Frontier of the United States in the Years 1814 and 1815. Philadelphia: Thomas Dobson, 1816.

Perkins, S. *A History of the Political and Military Events of the Late War Between the United States and Great Britain*. New Haven, CT: S. Converse, 1825.

"Proceedings and Debates of the House of Representatives of the United States." 12th Congress, 1st Session (1812). U.S. Government Records.

Ripley, E.A. *Facts Relative to the Campaign on the Niagara in 1814*. Boston: Self-published, 1815.

Sturtevant, I. *Barbarities of the Enemy Exposed in a report of the Committee of the House of Representatives of the United States*. Worcester, MA: Remark Dunnell, 1814.

Thomson, J.L. *Historical Sketches of the Late War Between the United States and Great Britain*. Philadelphia: Thomas Delsilver, 1816.

Wilkinson, J. *Diagrams and Plans Illustrative of the Principal Battles of the War of 1812*. Philadelphia: Self-published, 1815.

SECONDARY SOURCES

Later Secondary Publications

Baylies, N. *Eleazer Wheelock Ripley, of the War of 1812.* Des Moine, IA: Brewster & Co., 1890.

Blakeslee, S. *Narrative of Colonel Samuel Blakeslee; A Defender of Buffalo in the War of 1812.* Buffalo, NY: Buffalo Historical Society Publications, 1905.

Buell, W. *Military Movements in Eastern Ontario during the War of 1812.* Ontario Historical Society, Papers and Records, Vol. 10 (1913) and Vol. 17 (1919).

Cannon, R. *Historical Record of the 1st or Royal Regiment of Foot.* London, UK: William Clowes & Sons, 1847.

_____. *Historical Record of the Eighth or the Kings Regiment of Foot.* London, UK: Harrison & Co. Printers, 1844.

Carnochan, Janet. *Reminiscences of Niagara and St. David's.* Niagara Historical Society, Paper No. 20 (1911).

Cruickshank, Ernest. *Campaigns of 1812–1814.* Niagara Historical Society, Paper No. 9, 1902.

_____. *Letters of 1812 from the Dominion Archives.* Niagara Historical Society, Paper No. 23, 1913.

_____. *A Memoir of Colonel the Honourable James Kerby, His Life in Letters.* Welland County Historical Society, Papers and Records, No. 4, 1931.

Dorsheimer, W. *The Village of Buffalo during the War of 1812.* Presentation to the Buffalo Historical Society, 1863.

Douglass, D.B. "An Original Narrative of the Niagara Campaign." *The Historical Magazine,* Vol II, Third Series, 1873. Buffalo & Erie County Historical Society.

Edgar, M. *Ten Years in Upper Canada in Peace & War, 1805–1815: Being the Ridout Letters with Annotations by Matilda Edgar.* Toronto: William Brigs, 1890.

"Family History and Reminiscences of Early Settlers and Recollections of the War of 1812." Niagara Historical Society, Paper No. 28, 1915.

Government of the United States. *Causes of the Failure of the Army on the Northern Frontier.* Report to the House of Representatives, February 2, 1814, 13th Congress, 2nd Session, Military Affairs.

"Historic Houses." Niagara Historical Society, Paper No. 5, 1899.

Jay, W. "Table of the Killed and Wounded in the War of 1812." Ithaca, NY: New York State Historical Monographs, Historical Literature Collection, Cornell University Library.

Johnson, Frederick H. *A Guide for Every Visitor to Niagara Falls.* Niagara Falls, ON: Self-published, 1852.

"Journal of Mrs. Olivia Mitchell, Read before the Buffalo Historical Society January 10, 1881." Extract from the *Buffalo Courier,* January 11, 1881.

Kearsley, Major J. "The Memoirs of Major John Kearsley: A Michigan Hero from the War of 1812." *Military History Journal* 10 (May 1985). Clement Library, University of Michigan.

Kilborn, John. "Accounts of the War of 1812." In, Thaddeus W.H. Leavitt. *History of Leeds and Grenville Counties from 1749 to 1879.* Brockville, ON: Recorder Press, 1879.

Leavitt, T.W.H. *History of Leeds and Grenville Counties from 1749 to 1879.* Brockville, ON: Recorder Press, 1879.

Lossing, Benson. *Pictorial Field Book of the War of 1812.* New York: Harper and Brothers, 1868.

Niagara Historical Society Papers, Numbers 2, 3, 4, 5, 9, 11, 20, 22, 23, 28, 30, 31, 33. Niagara Historical Society.

Recollections of the Late Hon. James Crooks. Niagara Historical Society Papers, No. 28, (1916).

"Reminiscences of Arthur Galloway." Ithaca, NY: Cornell University Library.

"Reminiscences of Niagara." Niagara Historical Society, Paper No. 11 (1904).

Scott, Winfield. *Memoirs of Lieut. General Scott.* New York: Sheldon & Co., 1864. State Historical Monographs, Historical Literature Collection, Anonymous collection, circa 1850.

Severence, F.H., ed. *Papers Relating to the War of 1812 on the Niagara Frontier.* Buffalo Historical Society Publications, No. 5 (1902).

Smith, Perry H., ed. *History of the City of Buffalo & Erie Country Vol. 1*. Syracuse, NY: D. Mason & Co, 1884.

Warner, Robert I. *Memoirs of Capt. John Lampman and His Wife Mary Secord*. Welland County Historical Society, Papers and Records 3, 126–34 (1927).

Wright, Ross Pier. *The Burning of Dover*. Unpublished manuscript, 1948.

Books

Adams, Henry. *History of the United States of America during the Administrations of Madison*. New York: Library of America, 1986. Reprint of original 1891 volumes.

Antal, Sandy. *Invasions, Taking and Retaking Detroit and the Western District during the War of 1812*. Essex County Historical Society, 2011.

_____. *A Wampum Denied, Proctor's War of 1812*. Ottawa: Carleton University Press, 1997.

Auchinleck, George. *A History of the War Between Great Britain and the United States of America during the Years 1812, 1813 & 1814*. Toronto: Thomas Maclear, 1853. Reprint by Arms & Armour Press and Pendragon House, 1972.

Babcock, Louis L. *The War of 1812 on the Niagara Frontier, Volume 29*. Buffalo, NY: Buffalo Historical Society Publications, 1927.

Benn, Carl. *The Iroquois in the War of 1812*. Toronto: University of Toronto Press, 1998.

Bingham, Robert. W. *The Cradle of the Queen City: A History of Buffalo to the Incorporation of the City, Volume 31*. Buffalo, NY: Buffalo Historical Society Publications, 1931.

Blakeley, B. and MacDonald, C. *Norfolk, Haldimand and the War of 1812, Including the Six Nations*. Nanticoke, ON: Heronwood Enterprises, 2008.

Bowler, R. Arthur, ed. *War Along the Niagara, Essays on the War of 1812 and its Legacy*. Youngstown, NY: Old Fort Niagara Association, 1991.

Brant, Irving. *The Fourth President: A Life of James Madison*. Indianapolis & New York: The Bobbs Merrill Company, 1970.

Casselman, Alexander C., ed. *Richardson's War of 1812*. Toronto: Historical Publishing Co., 1902. Facsimile edition by Coles Publishing Co., Toronto, 1974.

Cruikshank, Ernest. *The Documentary History of the Campaigns upon the Niagara Frontier in 1812-1814*. 9 volumes. Welland, ON: Tribune Press, 1896–1908.

Dunnigan, Brian Leigh. *Forts Within a Fort, Niagara's Redoubts*. Youngstown NY: Old Fort Niagara Association Inc. 1989.

_____. *History and Development of Old Fort Niagara*. Youngstown NY: Old Fort Niagara Association Inc., 1985.

Elliott, C. *Winfield Scott, the Soldier and the Man*. Toronto: Macmillan, 1937.

Gardiner, Robert, ed. *The Naval War of 1812*. London, UK: Caxton Publishing Group, 2001.

Gayler, Hugh J., ed. *Niagara's Changing Landscapes*. Ottawa: Carleton University Press, 1994.

Gourlay, Robert. *Statistical Account of Upper Canada Compiled with a View to a Grand System of Emigration*. 2 Volumes. London, UK: Simpkin and Marshall, 1822. Republished by the Social Science Research Council of Canada, S.R. Publishers Ltd., Johnson Reprint Corp, 1966.

Graves, D.E. *Fix Bayonets! A Royal Welch Fusilier at War 1796-1815*. Montreal: Robin Brass Studio, 2006.

Graves, D.E., ed. *Soldiers of 1814, American Enlisted Men's Memoirs of the Niagara Campaign*. Youngstown, NY: Old Fort Niagara Association Inc. Lawrenceville, NJ: Princeton Academic Press, 1995.

Hitsman, J. Mackay. *The Incredible War of 1812: A Military History*. Toronto: Robin Brass Studio, 1999. Revised edition, updated by Donald Graves.

Horsman, R. *The Causes of the War of 1812*. New York: A.S. Barnes and Co., 1962.

Hough, Franklin B. *A History of St. Lawrence and Franklin Counties, New York*. Albany, NY: Little & Co., 1853.

Illustrated Historical Atlas of the Counties of Hastings & Prince Edward. Toronto: H. Belden & Co., 1878.

Illustrated Historical Atlas of the Counties of Lincoln and Welland. Toronto: H.R. Page, 1876.

Illustrated Historical Atlas of Norfolk County. Toronto: H. Belden & Co., 1877.

Irving, L.H. *Officers of the British Forces in Canada during the War of 1812.* Toronto: Canadian Military Institute, 1908.

Jarvis Papers. Women's Canadian Historical Society of Toronto Papers and Transactions, Transaction No. 5 (1902), 3–9.

Johnston, Winston. *The Glengarry Light Infantry, 1812–1816: Who Were They and What Did They Do in the War?* Self-published, 2011.

Klinck, Carl F. *Journal of Major John Norton.* Toronto: Champlain Society of Canada, Publication No. 46, 1970.

Lardas, Mark. *Great lakes Warships 1812–1815.* London, UK: Osprey Publishing, 2012.

Mackay, J. *The Incredible War of 1812.* Toronto: University of Toronto, 1965.

_____. *Lords of the Lake: The Naval War on Lake Ontario, 1812–1814.* Toronto: Robin Brass Studio, 1998.

Malcomson, Robert. *Warships of the Great Lakes, 1754–1834.* Rochester, UK: Chatham Publishing, 2001.

Nicholson, Colonel G.W.L. *The Fighting Newfoundlander: A History of the Royal Newfoundland Regiment.* Government of Newfoundland, 1963.

Ruttan, Henry. *Reminiscences of the Hon. Henry Ruttan: Loyalist Narratives from Upper Canada.* Toronto: Champlain Society, 1946.

Stagg, J.C.A. *Mr. Madison's War: Politics, Diplomacy, and Warfare in the Early American Republic 1783–1830.* Princeton, NJ: Princeton University Press, 1983.

Stanley, George F.G. *The War of 1812: Land Operations.* Toronto: Macmillan and the Canadian War Museum, 1983.

Stott, Glenn. *Greater Evils: The War of 1812 in Southwestern Ontario.* Self-published, 2001.

Wood, William C.H. *Select British Documents of the War of 1812.* 3 Volumes. Toronto: Champlain Society of Canada, 1920.

Wright, Ross Pier. *The Burning of Dover.* Erie, PA: Unpublished manuscript, 1948.

INDEX

Allison, Lieutenant, 94

Amherstburg, 15, 22, 42, 43, 48, 60

Ancaster, 15, 43, 91, 95

Anthony, Captain Charles, 74

Appling, Major Daniel, 86

Armstrong, U.S. Secretary of War Major General John, 16, 35, 37–38, 41, 63–67, 99–102

Armstrong, Lieutenant Richard, 120, 124, 129

Austin, Lieutenant Jonathan, 44–45

Baby, Lieutenant Colonel Francois, 47

Basden, Captain James, 50–51, 53–55, 57–58

Bathurst, Earl (Lord), 28, 33

Battle of Lake Erie, 18

Battle of the Thames/Moravianstown, 18, 42

Baynes, Colonel Edward, 81–82

Beaver Dams, 17

Bissell, Brigadier General David, 41

Black Ash Swamp, 60

Black Rock, 15, 16, 18, 91, 102, 110

Bostwick, Lieutenant John, 44–45

Boyd, Brigadier General John, 41

Brady, Colonel Hugh, 99

Brigham, Captain Belah B., 47

Britain, Royal Navy, 32, 68, 74

British Army, Canadian Fencible Regiments
Glengarry Light Infantry Fencible Regiment, 74, 77, 80
Royal Newfoundland Fencible Regiment, 109

British Army, Regular Army Regiments
1st (Royal Scots) Regiment, 11, 47, 49–50, 53, 55, 58, 108–09, 117, 118, 121–22, 124, 125, 127, 129, 131, 132, 135
8th (King's) Regiment, 11, 27, 103, 108–09, 110, 117, 118, 121–22, 124, 125, 127, 129, 131–33, 135
19th Light Dragoons, 94, 105, 108–09, 112, 117–18, 20, 124, 125, 127, 131, 133, 135
41st Regiment, 11, 109
89th Regiment, 11, 47, 49–50, 53, 58, 109
100th Regiment, 46, 103, 108, 110, 117, 118, 120, 124, 125, 127, 129, 131, 132, 135
Corps of Royal Artillery Drivers, 108–09

Royal Artillery Regiment, 74, 108–09, 110, 124
Royal Engineers Regiment, 74, 108
Royal Sappers and Miners, 74

British Naval Regiments
Royal Marine Artillery, 29, 74, 108
Royal Marines, 2, 29, 74, 77, 79, 82, 87

British Native allies, 118, 122, 123, 125, 138

Brock, Major General Isaac, 17

Brown, Major General Jacob, 40–41, 63–67, 87–88, 89, 93–94, 96, 98–102, 111, 113, 117–18, 121–23, 124, 125, 132–33, 135, 140, 141, 142, 146–47

Buck, Major Thomas, 103, 105, 107, 108

Buffalo, 15, 16, 18, 44, 63, 67, 69, 88, 89, 91–92, 96, 102, 115, 128

Burlington Heights, 15, 17, 18, 43, 44, 59, 91, 95, 101, 109, 146

Burton, Lieutenant, 94

Butler, Lieutenant Colonel Anthony, 48, 60

Caldwell, Captain William (Caldwell's Rangers), 50–51

Caldwell, Captain William "Billy" (Native allies), 50

Calibri, 32

Campbell, Senator George (U.S. Treasury), 38

Campbell, Colonel John B., 93, 96, 99

Campbell, Junior Puisne Justice William, 96

Charlotteville (Turkey Point), 94

Charwell, HMS, 32, 74

Châteauguay, 15, 16, 18

Chatham (U.K.), 32

Chauncey, Commodore Isaac, 28, 33, 35–36, 38–39, 63–64, 66–67, 83–84, 86–88, 100–02, 146–47

Chippawa, 15, 91, 102, 109–13, 115–39, 140, 141, 142, 143–44, 146

Chippawa River, 110–11, 113, 115, 116, 133, 140, 141, 142, 146

Chunn, Captain John, 94

Claus, William, 110

Cleopatra, 68

Cochrane, Vice Admiral Alexander, 96–97

Collier, Commander Edward, 74

Conquest, 35

Crooker, Captain, 112

Crossroads (Virgil), 12, 18, 91

Cruttenden, Captain Edwin, 74

Crysler, 31

Crysler's Farm, 15–16, 18, 42, 110

Dallaba, Major, 65

Delaware, 24, 42, 43, 47, 49–51, 53, 60

Detroit (MI), 15, 16, 17–18, 23, 42, 43, 47–48, 51, 60, 95, 102

Dickson, Lieutenant Colonel Thomas, 117

Dobbs, Captain Alexander, 74

Dolsen, Lieutenant John, 47

Dover Mills, 45, 94

Drummond, Lieutenant General Gordon,

20–24, 26–27, 47, 68–75, 80–83, 87–88, 94–96, 110, 135, 137, 139

Earl of Moria, 32, 74

Elliott, Lieutenant Colonel Matthew (BID), 50

Embargo Bill, 38

Erie (PA) (*see* Presque Isle)

Evans, Major Thomas, 117

Fair American, 35

Fenton, Colonel James, 93

Fischer, Lieutenant Colonel Victor, 74, 77, 80

Forks of the Thames (Chatham), 43, 48

Fort Amherstburg (Fort Malden), 15

Fort Chippawa, 24

Fort Erie, 15, 17, 24, 91, 102, 105, 107, 108, 110–11, 115, 118, 120

Fort George, 15, 16, 17–18, 26, 91, 100, 108, 109, 115, 144, 146

Fort Henry (*see* Point Henry)

Fort Meigs, 15, 17, 43

Fort Michilimackinac (Fort Mackinac), 15, 22

Fort Mississauga, 15, 24, 26, 91, 108

Fort Niagara, 15, 16, 18, 24, 26, 38, 63–65, 71, 91, 100, 108, 144

Fort Oswego (previously Fort Ontario), 15, 76, 79

Fort Schlosser, 15, 91

Fort Tompkins, 15, 35

Fort Volunteer, 15, 35

Fort York, 15, 17, 43

Fredericksburg, 80, 83–84

French Mills, 15, 35, 39–40, 63

Frenchman's Creek, 16, 17, 91, 12

Fulmer/Fuller, John, 48

Gaines, Brigadier General Edmund, 41, 67, 69

Galloway, Major Fenton, 94

Gardner, Adjutant General, 122–23, 125

General Pike, 35

Geneva (NY), 67

Georgian Bay, 33

Ghent (Belgium), 39

Gill, Captain William, 48, 51

Gordon, Lieutenant Colonel John, 117

Goshawk, 32

Gosset, Lieutenant William, 74

Grafton, Major Joseph, 99, 117

Grand River, 95

Granger, Lieutenant Colonel Erastus, 117

Granger, Lieutenant Colonel, 99

Growler, 77

Halifax, 29, 96

Hall, Lieutenant James, 132, 135

Hamilton, Lieutenant Colonel Christopher, 15, 17, 108

Harris, Captain Samuel D., 99, 117

Hay, Lieutenant Colonel George (Marquis of Tweedale), 117

Head-of-the-Lake (Hamilton), 17

Hindman, Major Jacob, 99, 117

Holmes, Captain Andrew Hunter, 48–49, 51, 56, 59–60

Horton, Lieutenant, 112

Howard, Captain George, 109

Hull, Brigadier General William, 17

Izard, Major General George, 41

Jackson, Lieutenant George, 47, 51

Jefferson, 69

Jesup, Major Thomas, 96, 99, 117, 131

Johnstone, Captain David, 50

Jones, 69

Jones, U.S. Secretary of the Navy William, 36–38

Julia, 35

Kingston, 15, 22–23, 26–27, 29–30, 32–33, 36, 63–67, 69, 71, 74, 81, 87, 95–96, 146

Lacolle Mills (Lower Canada), 41
Lais, 68
Larwell/Larwill, Lieutenant, 45
Leavenworth, Major Henry, 99, 117
Lee, Captain, 48, 51
Lewis, Major General Morgan, 41
Lewiston, 15, 91, 144, 146
Lisle, Major Robert, 117
London (England), 39
Long Point, 22, 24, 42, 43, 62, 91, 93–95, 101–02, 109
Longwoods, 15, 43, 50–51, 54–55, 61
Lord Beresford, 32
Lord Melville, 32, 74
Lord Nelson, 31
Lundy's Lane, 91, 116
Lyon's Creek, 141, 142, 143

Mackinac Island, 15
Macomb, Colonel Alexander , 41
Maconochie, Captain James, 117
Madison, 35
Madison, President James, 13, 16, 38
Magnet, 32, 74
Malcolm, Lieutenant Colonel, 74, 77
Malden (*see* Amherstburg)
Mallory, Lieutenant Colonel Benajah, 45
Markle, Abraham, 94
Martin, Major, 94
McCrea, Thomas, 45–46
McDonald, Lieutenant, 94, 121
McFarland, Major Daniel, 99, 117
McGregor, Lieutenant/Captain John, 45, 50
McMillan, Captain Alexander, 74
McNeil, Major John, 117
Medcalf, Lieutenant Henry, 45–46

Michilimackinac (Mackinac), 15, 102
Miles, Ensign Francis, 58
Miller, Lieutenant Colonel James, 99
Mitchell, Lieutenant Colonel George, 76, 80
Mohawk, 69, 83
Monroe, U.S. Secretary of State James, 38
Montreal, 15, 18, 27, 32, 38, 39
Montreal, 74
Moravianstown (Fairfield), 15, 42, 43, 49
Mulcaster, Captain William, 74, 77

Nanticoke Creek, 44
Napoleon Bonaparte, 38
Nelly, 68
Newark (Niagara-on-the-Lake), 12, 15, 17, 18, 91, 100, 144
Niagara, 31, 32, 74
Non-Intercourse Bill, 38
Norton, Captain John (Teyoninhokarawen), 108, 110, 117, 118, 120–21, 140
Nottawasaga River, 33

O'Conor, Captain Richard, 74
Ogdensburg, 15
Oswego, 15, 69, 73, 75, 76–88
Owen, Commander Charles, 74
Oxford (Beamsville-Ingersoll), 42, 43, 62

Patterson's Creek (Lynn River), 94
Pearce, Lieutenant George, 76
Pearson, Lieutenant Colonel Thomas, 110–12, 115, 122, 141, 142
Penelope, 77
Pert, 35
Pike, Brigadier General Zebulon, 63
Pinkney, Colonel Ninian, 82
Plattsburg, 15, 40, 81
Point Frederick, 29, 30, 32, 68
Popham, Captain Stephen, 74, 87

Port Dover, 15, 42, 43, 46, 91, 93–94
Port Talbot, 42, 43, 45, 48, 60, 62, 95
Porter, Brigadier General Peter B., 93, 99, 102–03, 117, 120–22, 132–33
Powell, Senior Puisne Judge William, 96
Poyntz, Lieutenant Newdigate, 33
Prescott, 15, 27, 71, 110
Presque Isle (Erie, PA), 15, 43
Prevost, Sir George, 21–24, 26, 28, 33, 35, 70–75, 81–83, 96–97, 110, 135, 137
Prince Regent, 31, 32, 68, 74
Princess Charlotte, 31, 68, 74
Prompte, 32
Psyche, 32
Put-in-Bay, 15, 22, 43
Putnam's Creek, 11

Queenston, 15, 16, 17, 24, 91, 108, 115, 144, 146
Queenston, 31

Riall, Major General Phineas, 26, 59–60, 62, 95–96, 105, 109, 111, 113, 115, 117–18, 120, 122–23, 128, 131–32, 135–37, 139, 140, 141, 142, 144, 146
Rice, Lieutenant Moses, 45
Ripley, Brigadier General Eleazer W., 41, 99, 100–03, 117, 132, 141, 142
Robinson, Captain (brevet Lieutenant Colonel) William, 27
Rondeau, 43, 48
Ropes, Captain Benjamin, 117, 123, 124, 125, 127, 128, 131, 135
Royal George, 32, 74

Sackets Harbor, 15, 17, 28, 31, 33, 36–37, 39–40, 63, 67, 68–69, 71–72, 74–75, 76, 81–83, 85, 87–88, 89, 92, 100–01
Sandwich (Windsor), 15, 17, 43
Sandy Creek, 85, 86–87

Scott, Chief Justice Thomas, 95

Scott, Brigadier General Winfield, 41, 64–65, 89–91, 93, 96, 98, 99, 100, 102–03, 107, 112–13, 117, 121, 123, 127–29, 141

Secord, Laura, 17

Sheaffe, Major General Roger Hale, 17

Sheppard, Lieutenant Edward, 120, 124

Sinclair, Commander Arthur, 93

Sir Sydney Smith, 32

Sovereign's Mills, 91

Spilsbury, Captain Francis, 74

Springer, Captain Daniel, 47

St. Davids, 91

St. Lawrence, 31, 87

St. Petersburg (Russia), 39

Star, 32, 74

Stevens, Lieutenant, 74

Stewart, Captain (brevet Lieutenant Colonel) Alexander, 50, 53–54, 59–60, 109

Stoney Creek, 15, 16, 17

Stonington (CT), 97

Superior, 69, 83, 84, 87

Swift, Brigadier General Joseph, 41

Sylph, 35

Talbot, Colonel Thomas, 93–95

Tecumseh (Leaping Panther), 17, 18

Teyoninhokarawen (*see* Norton, Captain John)

Thames River, 18, 42, 47–48, 49

Three River Point, 80

Towson, Captain Nathaniel, 127

Treat, Captain Joseph, 120

Turkey Point (*see* Charlotteville)

Twenty Mile Creek, 49, 51, 53

Upper Canada Militia Regiments

   1st Kent County Embodied Militia Regiment (aka Loyal Kent Volunteers), 45, 47, 49, 59

1st Middlesex County Embodied Militia Regiment, 47

1st Norfolk County Embodied Militia Regiment, 44

1st Oxford County Embodied Militia Regiment (Rifle Company), 47

2nd Essex County Embodied Militia Regiment (aka Loyal Essex Volunteers), 60

2nd Lincoln County Embodied Militia Regiment, 117, 118, 120, 122

2nd Norfolk County Embodied Militia Regiment, 44–45

Provincial Light Cavalry (Dragoons) Regiment, 45, 108, 109

Runchie's Coloured Corps, 108

Volunteer Battalion of Incorporated Militia of Upper Canada (Artillery), 27, 146

Volunteer Battalion of Incorporated Militia of Upper Canada (Infantry), 27, 146

Western Rangers, 49, 53

Ussher farmstead, 128, 140, 141, 142

U.S. Army, Regular Regiments

   Ninth Regiment, 99, 112, 117, 127, 128, 131, 132, 135

   Eleventh Regiment, 99, 117, 127, 128–29, 131, 132, 135

   Nineteenth Regiment, 93, 94, 117

   Twenty-First Regiment, 98, 99, 117, 120, 123, 124, 125, 128, 131, 135

   Twenty-Second Regiment, 94, 99, 117, 127, 128, 131, 132, 135

   Twenty-Third Regiment, 99, 117

   Twenty-Fourth Regiment, 51, 53, 94

   Twenty-Fifth Regiment, 99, 107, 110, 117, 127, 128–29, 131, 135

   Twenty-Sixth Regiment, 45, 94

   Twenty-Seventh Regiment, 94

Canadian Volunteers, 44, 94, 99

U.S. Marine Corps, 94

U.S. Native Allies, 99, 117, 138

U.S. State Militia Regiments

   Fifth Pennsylvania State Volunteer Regiment, 99, 117

   Twenty-Fourth Tennessee State Militia Regiment, 51, 53

   Twenty-Sixth Vermont State Militia Regiment, 51, 53, 58

   Twenty-Seventh New York State Volunteer Regiment, 51, 53, 58

   Twenty-Eighth Kentucky State Militia Regiment, 51, 53

   Michigan Militia Dragoons, 48, 51, 53

   Michigan Rangers, 47, 48, 51, 53

   Pennsylvania State Volunteer Regiment (unspecified), 93, 94

Victory, HMS, 31

Virgil (*see* Crossroads)

Washington, D.C., 97

Weishoun's Point, 91, 116, 141, 142, 143

Westbrook, Andrew, 47, 95

Wilkinson, Alexander, 48

Wilkinson, Major General James, 40–41

Willcocks, Major William, 99

Winder, Brigadier General William H., 70, 82

Wolfe, 32, 74

Wood, Major Eleazar, 96

Wood, Major James, 117

Woolsey, Commandant Melancthon, 77, 84, 86–87

Yeo, Sir James, 22, 26–29, 31–33, 36, 68–75, 78, 80–81, 84, 87–88

York (Toronto), 15, 17, 27, 29, 43, 45, 69, 71, 95, 109, 115, 144, 146

FROM THE SAME SERIES

The Call to Arms
The 1812 Invasions of Upper Canada
Richard Feltoe
9781459704398
$19.99

The Call to Arms is the first of six books in the series Upper Canada Preserved — War of 1812. Each book in this battlefield-based chronicle combines the best of modern historical research with extensive quotations from original official documents and personal letters to bring to life this crucial period of Canada's early history. Numerous historical images of locations are counterpointed with comparable modern perspectives to give a true then-and-now effect. Custom-drawn maps are also included to trace the course of individual battles stage-by-stage, while placing and moving the shifting formations of troops across a geographically accurate battlefield.

In this first entry in the series, the focus is on the 1812 invasions of Upper Canada: the Battles of Detroit, Queenston Heights, and Frenchman's Creek, and features such figures as Major General Isaac Brock, Brigadier General William Hull, Major General Roger H. Sheaffe, and Tecumseh, among others.

Available at your favourite bookseller

Visit us at
Dundurn.com | @dundurnpress | Facebook.com/dundurnpress | Pinterest.com/dundurnpress